THE
WEALTH
BLUEPRINT

A GUIDE TO FINANCIAL MASTERY
FOR PROFESSIONALS AND ENTREPRENEURS

DEVIN ALPHIN

DEDICATION

Thank you creator for allowing me to be exposed to this knowledge, and the experiences I've had both positive and negative. Thank you for giving me this assignment and the gifts to complete it.

To my family, I thank each one of you for the lessons you've taught me. Thank you all for your love and support.

Thank you Dawn for investing in me. Thank you Joe for the conversations, notes and taking the time.

Thank you to everyone who contributed to the completion of this book and to everyone who reads and implements even one thing from it.

Grateful!

TABLE OF CONTENTS

INTRODUCTION

It became apparent to me quickly that leaving that room unscathed would be more challenging than I had thought. I had no idea how much of a turning point in my life this one day in August of 2017 would end up being.

I sat at that table, face to face with a woman who didn't know me from Adam, yet made every assumption she could about me. No pleasantries, just business, as she proceeded to run down the list of every unpaid bill with an undertone of disgust, as if to paint me as an irresponsible adult, and even parent. All this, just to be approved for Chapter 13 bankruptcy.

I was 28 at the time.

I didn't get there by pure irresponsibility. I got there by doing my best to take care of my family. Still, I couldn't help the feeling that my best wasn't good enough.

As a husband, father, and primary income earner, managing life was overwhelming. Looking back now, I acknowledge that I did not have the tools or a plan. I just jumped in, relying solely on the belief that I could figure it out. I was 21.

Families have needs. Vehicles break down. Kids get sick and need to go to the emergency room. Houses need maintenance.

You get the point. There were times I just wanted to see my kids smile, times I wanted to please my wife, times we wanted to have fun for once, and so I spent the money, knowing I probably shouldn't have.

There's only so long you can rob Peter to pay Paul before Peter goes broke too. Bankruptcy became my best option. As men, the responsibility of providing for our families is closely tied to our sense of manhood and confidence. It left me more than embarrassed, I was ashamed. Deep feelings of inadequacy and failure, after a long road of financial struggle and trauma, became the icing on the cake.

But at the same time, it was a blessing in disguise. I would use the next five years to pay that bankruptcy down, to learn hard lessons about money, and ultimately, to choose to have my bankruptcy dismissed. Throughout that entire period, my career also began to move in a different direction.

After becoming a father at 20, and not wanting to go into any more student loan debt, I chose to drop out. Needing to provide, I put on a suit and walked into a bank looking for a job. The branch manager was a woman who, I believe, saw my light. She looked me over and, without hesitation, said, "I like your drive. Come back Monday. You've got a job as a bank teller." That following Monday, in late 2011 at the age of 22, was the start of my career in finance, a field I knew nothing about and had not gone to school for.

After a year as a bank teller and two gunpoint robberies, I realized that being behind the bank counter was not where I wanted to be. I wanted to do what those bankers in the lobby did, the ones who had seats instead of standing all day. So my career progressed from behind the counter as a bank teller to a desk in the lobby as a banker, working with individuals and their accounts.

It was better, but working from 8:30 to 6:30, plus some Saturdays, with a young family, was a grind. The money was better, but not great, and I was unfulfilled. While working at the bank, I noticed a gentleman who also worked for the bank but seemed to walk in and out as he pleased. His fresh suits, commanding presence, and polished demeanor intrigued me. When he came in, he would head straight to the back, meet with his clients, and then leave for the day.

Eventually, I made friends with him and learned what he did. He told me he was a financial advisor and dealt with investments.

"What's it take to do that?" I asked.

"Licenses," he said.

I began to shadow him and learn the ropes. After referring bank business to him and proving myself for a while, the branch manager at my bank, another woman, who I am grateful saw my light, asked if I'd be interested in getting my own investment licenses. If so, management would pay for the education.

I spent the next few months studying late at night and eventually passed the tests to acquire the first round of licenses needed to become a financial advisor associate, a junior advisor, if you will.

I did that for two years but needed more licenses before I could drop the "associate" title and become a full advisor on my own.

More late-night studying, more tests, more licenses.

I was now a 25-year-old financial advisor responsible for all of the investment activity of five bank branches.

By this time, we'd had our second son. And while the official title of Financial Advisor was nice, the money never seemed to be enough. Still the primary earner, I struggled with the basics. Again, I realize now it was my lack of tools, knowledge, and planning that kept me stuck in that loop.

The time for me to make a decision had long passed. The combination of both my wife and desperation pushed me to apply for a position that I felt was way out of my reach. The description read as if 10 years of experience, at the very least, was required.

Over the next four long months, while scraping by, I went through a seven-interview hiring process, ultimately beating out applicants I know were more qualified than I was. All of this was to become a Wealth Manager at a Fortune 500 company that handled high-net-worth individuals' accounts and retirement planning.

What's for you is for you.

More studying, more tests, more licenses.

Imagine a baby-faced 26-year-old Black male college dropout, sitting across the desk in a metro Atlanta high-rise from a

70-year-old white cardiologist with a decorated career, ready to retire, and telling him what to do with his millions.

I still remember hiding my nervousness by wiggling my toes frantically. All business up top, above the desk, but a wreck below. I look back and laugh.

My career progressed quickly, but my finances and inner confidence deteriorated at the same pace. Bankruptcy, young parenthood, and the stress of it all in marriage took their toll. I lost weight, dealt with my share of denial and depression, and honestly spent years feeling like a shell of myself. All while putting on a mask to perform at work.

I realize now how I allowed myself to become a victim of life. But at the time, I couldn't help asking, why?

Why is this happening? Why is it so hard? Why isn't this seeming to get any better?

Bankruptcy helped give me some of my answers. It taught me valuable lessons about money that the books didn't. Ultimately, we were able to pay off over $55,000 in debt while saving five figures in retirement funds. Toward the end of the bankruptcy, we actually went to the court and chose to have it dismissed rather than finishing it, a choice that saved us $3,000.

Why did I tell you that story? I want you to know that I have both the personal experience of what not to do, as well as the career experience and knowledge of what to do. And that is why I wanted to create this book.

My intention with this book is to provide you with a blueprint on how to both manage money and build financial security for you and your family. Wealth is great, I see it every day, but you cannot create true wealth, which includes peace of mind, on a shaky foundation. There are seven pillars to building the foundation of wealth. This book is going to dive into each of them in basic, everyday language and provide you with practical steps you can take to plan and create financial security.

This is a map for you to use. Regardless of your income level, the principles and information I'm going to provide will serve as a foundation for how to manage your money, whether it's hundreds or millions.

The great author Bell Hooks said it best: "Education is one of the greatest forms of therapy." Until we acknowledge and heal our personal financial trauma, the scarcity mindset will lurk at the root of our financial decisions, affecting our peace of mind. Regardless of your net worth or account balances, that is not true wealth. So hopefully, this book can serve as a little bit of financial trauma therapy for you as well, if needed.

This book is not going to make you rich. It's not going to do the work for you. Nor will it reinvent the wheel. Everything I'm going to share is public knowledge, and I encourage you to do your own research. However, I will be able to put the pieces of the puzzle together in a way that will hopefully resonate with you.

By the end of this book, you will have a deep understanding of how every aspect of your finances fits together. You will gain confidence and authority over your money, and you will have the knowledge and tools to build true, lasting wealth.

In short, you will have *The Wealth Blueprint.* Let's get started.

CHAPTER I

MENTALITY SHAPES REALITY

Belief

1. Something that is **accepted, considered** to be true, or held as an **opinion**.

2. A **habit** of mind in which trust or confidence is placed in a person or thing.

"A belief is a thought you keep thinking" - Me

Money Scripts

What can you recall seeing, hearing and learning about money growing up?

There are studies that show that many of our core beliefs and habits dealing with money are set by the age of seven.

Things like planning ahead, prioritizing, returning borrowed items and delayed gratification are all things that we pick up either positive or negative habits around by the age of seven, and usually carry into adulthood. Whether you're mindful of them or not, they shape how you make financial decisions.

With that being said, those core systems of belief were studied by two financial psychologists, Ted and Brad Klontz, who famously grouped them into what are called, *Money Scripts*. There's four basic money scripts that just about everyone falls into.

When *Money Avoidance* is your script, there is an inherent belief at the root that money is in some way bad, or that they do not deserve wealth. Money avoiders often see the wealthy as greedy and corrupt. And believe that there is virtue in living with less. Because of this, they may often be their own worst enemy and sabotage their financial success by doing things such as avoiding their accounts and statements etc., giving money away, or financially enabling others all as subconscious attempts to avoid money.

Money Worshippers believe it's their key to happiness. More money equals more freedom and a better life in general. Ironically, they usually have lower net worths and higher credit card debt. Purchasing things in an attempt to achieve happiness is a tell tale sign. Money worshippers may put work ahead of family, but are never satisfied by the pursuit because they believe it's never enough.

The *Money Status* script is centered on the belief that your net worth is your self-worth. Subscribers to this script are usually given a sense of value by public signs of wealth, which make them prone to overspending and even being financially dependent on others. Keeping their spending patterns hidden from spouses or loved ones is a common theme as well. Growing up in poverty or lower income conditions are typically at the root of this script as those from higher income circumstances may have been put on a pedestal.

Finally, there's *Money Vigilance*. Those who are money vigilant believe that money should be saved, kept private and monitored on a regular basis. They have solid financial habits and seek a sense of security in having enough money. They don't typically buy on credit, nor do they keep secrets from their partners. When money vigilance is your script, the vigilance can creep into anxiety and excessive worry over your financial health- which can ultimately prevent you from enjoying your money. However, overall the vigilant are the healthiest of the scripts.

Be sure to identify which one or two resonate the most with you. No judgment, it's just about identifying where you are so that you can begin to be more mindful about your decisions in order to reshape your relationship with money.

FINANCIAL TRAUMA

We've also got to identify what's behind that money script. For many of us, it's financial trauma. Financial trauma is defined as the physical, emotional and/or cognitive impact we experience when trying to cope with an event or series of events around money. It could be something as deep as growing up in poverty, or as simple as overhearing your parents argue about money. It often shows up in your life as negative beliefs, over or under-spending, avoidance, anxiety and/ or depression, low self-esteem, or isolation from your relationships due to money. So, how do you heal that financial trauma?

Well, congratulations! Reading this book is one of those ways. Educating yourself is a great way to practice healing.

But to shift and release these deeply set beliefs and trauma you're going to have to do more than that! You're going to have to do some emotional work.

Have you ever written a forgiveness letter? A forgiveness letter is one that you write, by hand, either to yourself or to someone else that needs to be forgiven- for whatever it is that needs forgiving. I've written a few and when it came to my relationship with money, I had to forgive myself for a lot of things!

The concept of forgiveness is powerful, and often misunderstood. Did you know that the definition of forgiveness is, to stop the feelings of anger and resentment etc. against an offender? That's powerful because it's truly not about them, it's about you. You are the one carrying the negative emotions that are literally weighing you down and keeping you in a negative loop. By truly forgiving, you're stopping those feelings. What's deeper is that if you're holding those feelings toward yourself- you are divided within yourself, and a house divided against itself cannot stand.

I wrote that letter, took it in my backyard, dug a hole, dropped it in, burned it, watched it burn to the very last ash, then buried the ashes. Now, I'm not saying that immediately after doing that you're healed, but it definitely is a very powerful practice that shifts things at both a conscious and subconscious level. So are meditation and talking things out with a trusted person. Licensed professional or not, giving a voice to things with someone you trust is important because we are communal beings, especially throughout our history. We are meant to operate within a community, thus our tribal roots. So if you're operating solo and in silence, you're going to have a tough time growing beyond a certain point. These are all practices I suggest for healing financial trauma. However, I'm going to walk you through some additional powerful tools that can help provide clarity and direction. Let's start by clearly identifying, and writing your money vision.

Money Vision

You cannot be what you cannot see. I'm a big believer in metaphysics, and regardless of if you are or not, there's plenty of science that backs the power of envisioning in order to manifest a thing. But even more simple than that. Consider the fact that everything is created twice.

First in your mind, then in "real" life. So, if you want financial security, if you want to be wealthy, it first starts in your mind. You must be able to see and feel it. So, I'll ask you, what does your money vision look like? Where do you live? How do you earn your income? Who do you hang with? What does it feel like to be financially free? How do you spend your time? How do you eat? What's in your bank account? Where do you travel? How do you dress? What do you do for fun? All these things and more when combined equal your money vision.

Take the time to really envision and dream. Talk about it with your significant other. Now, **write it down by hand.** There's something so powerful about taking that vision, having it travel down your spine through your shoulder all the way out from your fingertips onto paper– then reading it back, out loud! It is a kinesthetic, auditory and visual experience. It doesn't get more real than that!

For years I carried my money vision in the glovebox of my car. It literally went everywhere with me!

When you have a vision, you have a target. As life happens, you can sit, close your eyes and call forth that vision. When you do, take care to truly feel what it's like to be in that space. Your subconscious mind doesn't know the difference between real life and the imagination. This is why an intense scene in a movie gets your adrenaline pumping as if it's real. So feel that vision, the deeper you do the more you call it forth in real life.

We learn, and create our lives through emotionally-charged repetition. So the more you do this, the more your thoughts, feelings, actions, relationships, and overall external circumstances will begin to align with that vision.

The vision is HUGE, but it's not all there is to creating the financial security you seek. The vision is your "what." It's what you desire; but, you have to know your "why." You see, to get from where you are now to where you want to be is going to require massive action. Motivation is great, and having the vision helps motivate you. But purpose is greater than motivation, because motivation will eventually fade. But a purpose, when crafted correctly, is bigger than you. So, it has enough power to keep you going even when motivation fades. Your whys are your anchor keeping you grounded in your purpose and vision. Take some time to really think about your whys

"I want to be rich," is not a why. "I want to be rich to be able to spend more time with my kids and make more memories," that's a why! Again, your whys should be bigger than you. So take some time to write down by hand your whys. You'll notice, even if it's hard at first, that the more you do it, more and more whys will begin to pop up as you go about your days.

So you've got your vision, which is what you want, and you know your whys. Now, how are you going to get there? This is where having financial goals really comes into play. These are the stepping stones along the way. When creating goals you want them to be S.M.A.R.T. If you're not familiar the acronym, S.M.A.R.T. stands for Specific, Measurable, Attainable, Relevant and Time-based.

I'll give you an example. I will save $30,000 for a down payment on my new home in two years. It's very specific. You can measure it. It is achievable. It's relevant to your situation. And it's based on a time limit. SMART goals help you check off the boxes along the way to realizing your vision.

AFFIRMATIONS

If you're anything like me, the sabotager in you WILL come out to play. Affirmations can help you stay in the driver's seat. The power of affirming yourself is not to be underestimated. Here are some affirmations that you can use to help keep you grounded and moving along the path to your financial vision.

- I am safe and secure regardless of the amount in my account
- I make wise decisions with money.

- I allow abundance.

- I allow wealth.

- Money flows easily to me.

- I am capable of overcoming any money obstacles that stand in my way.

- I am worthy of wealth.

- Every dollar I spend comes back to me multiplied.

Having your mindset aligned with your money vision is imperative. Yes, there are tools, knowledge and resources that you will need; which we're about to get into next. But they're all for nothing if scarcity mindset and fear rule you at a deep subconscious level. By taking the time and doing the consistent work on your mindset, you'll help yourself achieve those goals much faster. So, I encourage you. to identify your money script and your core beliefs about money; heal your financial trauma; write your vision; know your whys; have your S.M.A.R.T. goals; and stick to your affirmations along the way!

Now you're ready to start working on your cash flow! Let's go there next.

CHAPTER II

CASH FLOW MANAGEMENT

Making more money will not solve your problems if cash flow management is your issue. It will only make it worse.

When it comes to cash flow, there are five important things that you need:

- You need a plan for your income, no matter what the income is;
- Pay yourself first;
- You must know how to prioritize your spending;
- You need an emergency fund;
- And unless you're debt free, you need a debt strategy.

PLANNING YOUR INCOME

Why does the word "budget" have such a negative connotation? Most of the millionaires I've worked with are pretty clear about their budget, even the ones that are on pace to run out! They know roughly how much it takes to run their household on a monthly basis, they know about how much they usually spend on things like travel per year; they have an idea of what they'd like to pay when it's time for a new car, or upgrading their home etc. Of course things come up, and they may go over budget with certain situations, but they know their numbers for the most part.

However, it seems like those with less money associate budgeting with scarcity, stress and all things negative. This is for a few different reasons. Budgeting can seem complex and time consuming, and for little benefit. It can also be a reminder of your financial difficulties or even past negative experiences. I think one of the biggest reasons why is because it can also feel very restrictive. I've dealt with all of these, so there's no denying their validity. However, if you can approach budgeting with a new mindset, just for a little bit, and simplify the process; I promise, you'll see that budgeting will give you a transformational sense of control and peace of mind. Let me help you!

Let's stop using the "B" word. Instead let's use the word "plan." That's all it is at its core, is a plan for your dollars. Your dollars work for you, so give them a plan. You can adjust that plan however you see fit based on your priorities. You are in control. You can keep your plan in an app, a spreadsheet like me, or even write it on a napkin (although I wouldn't suggest that!). It's whatever works for you, but you've got to do it. After all, if you fail to plan, you plan to fail.

Keep your plan as simple as possible, especially when starting out. The more complex you get, the harder it is to stick to it. A simple plan to start with is the 50/30/20 plan. It's even easy to remember. 50/30/20 stands for 50% to your needs, 30% to your loves/ likes, and 20% for savings and debt.

Grab a sheet of paper to list all of your monthly expenses. Determine what's a need, a love and a like (more on this in a bit) and be sure to have savings and debt first. You've got to pay yourself first! That's another key in all of this. Why pay the light company before you pay yourself?

Now, what you may find is that your expenses don't line up perfectly with the 50/30/20. That's ok, adjust it for you. If right now your needs are 70%, that's ok. Just be really clear about what's a need, a love or a like. The numbers don't lie, so you may be confronted with some tough decisions about having to let go of some things. Congrats, now you're doing work! Your future self will thank you for making the short term sacrifice, for the long term money vision and goals you set. The more you can push toward your savings, the quicker you can accomplish those goals you set. Challenge yourself, but don't overly restrict yourself either. Be realistic. You need some fun and entertainment, you can't cut everything!

Now you've got a general framework of how to map your money out. Even if it is 70% needs, 20% wants, and 10% savings and debt. I wouldn't drop below that 10% on savings. If you do, make it a very temporary thing.

Also, to ensure you're saving, don't rely on discipline- instead rely on technology. What I mean is, **automate your saving.** For those employed, more often than not, your employer can split your direct deposit across multiple accounts. Simply have an amount or percentage going directly to your savings so you don't have to think about it or do it yourself, it's automatic. If your employer does not, or you are self- employed, your bank should be able to make automatic transfers for you. You can set it up right on your bank app in most cases at whatever frequency you'd like.

For those who are more detail oriented, or feeling comfortable and experienced with budgeting you can get deeper and have specific categories in your plan. For instance: 25% for Housing, 5% Personal expenses, etc. but don't get too far in the weeds if that's not you. Again, you want this to be simple so that: 1) It doesn't stress you out; 2) You can communicate clearly with your partner or spouse if in a relationship; and finally, 3) You can stick to it.

Speaking of communication, this is very important in relationships and it's an area I struggled for many years! I've recently found out why. Take a look at the following two communication styles and see which your partner can grasp easier:

"Babe, right now 70% of our income is covering our needs. We need to set a goal of how we can get that down to 60% so that we can have more going towards our savings and debt which is only at about 10% of our income right now. If we can do that, we'll have a better vacation budget at the beach."

OR

"Babe, right now we're spending $1700 on rent, $500 on groceries every two weeks, and I've got to cover more on the utilities this month since the A/C is running more. Also the kids need clothes for the summer by the end of the month. I haven't forgotten about the vacation later this year, but right now we're putting away about $150 a month and that's not going to cut it. We'd make it, but we'd be tight in Panama. If we can cut the bills back by about $100, we could put that in savings and..."

You get the point. Keep it simple, talk in percentages.

One final point in communication and cash management within a relationship is this- if your spouse is less emotionally attached to money; has healed or manages any financial trauma more effectively than you; or is simply better with managing the finances, ALLOW them to do it. This of course is if they are willing, and you two can establish clear boundaries and expectations on how that will work. Trust me, you'll save the both of you a lot of potential stress, and quite possibly your relationship. Considering the significant statistics on marriages ending in divorce, and money being one of the most common reasons for ending marriages, your ego is not worth it. Take a step back, empower your partner and allow them to assist while you work on your money mindset.

PAY YOURSELF FIRST

I could've been much farther in my life at this point if it didn't take me as long as it did to start paying myself first. It's one of the biggest habits you can develop and you will avoid a lot of pain while saving yourself years of clean up. No matter what, pay yourself first. Your future self, your family, and if you have children, will all thank you.

It's not even about how much you save, at least in the beginning. What matters is the habit and that can only be done through repetition. Because if you can't pay yourself a dollar, you won't pay yourself ten dollars. If not ten, definitely not a hundred or a thousand dollars either. We tell ourselves that we'll do it when we have enough, or after such and such is paid, but that's a flat out lie. Bills will always be there, no matter what income level or net worth you're at, there's bills. The reality goes back to those beliefs. You *believe* you can't afford to, and that there isn't enough to pay yourself first. What's even deeper is, let's say that is true; that means you don't have enough- **and,** you're giving it all to other people. Would you do that with the last of your water? Time and again, life will show you that you can't afford *not* to save.

As you start paying yourself first, you'll develop two things: pride and discipline. You'll set natural boundaries around that money because it means something to you.

I recently read a story about a man who had a terrible habit of biting his nails. He tried everything to break the habit, but nothing worked. His wife suggested getting a manicure. When he did, he loved how his nails looked; the manicurist complimented them and he took great pride in them. That pride was the shift that broke the habit for him.

Pay yourself first, no matter the amount and no matter what. You'll develop discipline and a sense of pride from knowing you've prioritized yourself and your financial well-being.

PRIORITIZING YOUR SPENDING

I challenge you to print out your bank statements for the last three months. Go through every expense and highlight the trends; whether it's eating out, shopping, or whatever. Why am I having you do that? It's so that you notice the trends in your spending; and because what doesn't get measured, doesn't improve. Add up how much you've spent in the last three months on whatever the trend(s) is/ are. You might be surprised, or even disgusted, like I was when I realized we had spent $3000 on eating out in a short time frame after I'd received a bonus from my job one year!

Just being aware starts the change, but here's the real challenge- can you cut that by even 10%? What if you cut it by 25% or 50%? How much more money would you have to go towards other areas of your plan, that may be more impactful. This is how you can begin to prioritize your spending and fueling those long-term goals and vision.

This is the second key of cash flow management. Having a plan is great, but you also need to know how to prioritize your spending. Luckily you've already begun within your money plan. Simply ask yourself, "do I **need** it, **love** it, or **like** it, before you swipe your card or press pay.

Often we get the impulse to buy things that we like. Whether we're scrolling or we're walking through the store, whatever the case, the "likes" pop up. The likes are shiny and a lot of times it's about the instant gratification. The likes also end up getting you in situations where you're short when it comes to the things you love, or even the things you need.

I'm not saying anything is wrong with the likes. I'm just saying you need to clearly identify. What is the need? What is a love? And what is a like? Nine times out of ten, your money vision is full of the things that you love; so if more of your dollars are going to the likes, less is going to your loves and your needs. You will have a more fulfilling life if you can prioritize. Building the habit of asking yourself that simple question will help tremendously.

EMERGENCY FUND

Next up is, you've got to have an emergency fund. It's not a matter of *if* life will happen, it's *when*. Right now, the average American is unable to cover a $400 emergency. There's no wonder why so many families are check to check and maxed out on credit cards. One hot water heater blowing; one transmission going out; one emergency plane ticket; one trip to the emergency room for your child is all it takes. That's why the emergency fund is so crucial. There's a golden rule of finance that you want to have anywhere from three to six months of living expenses in the bank in an account that you don't touch ready to be accessed when you need it. Revisit your money plan for a minute. When considering an emergency fund, it's typically not based on your full monthly expenses, it's based on what many folks would call your "noodle budget." If things are tight, what's still got to be paid? Multiply that by three to six months, then put it to the side and you're solid.

I wouldn't recommend keeping it in something that needs to be sold in order to get the cash, but somewhere that it's already liquid and readily accessible. Also, the three to six months really just depends on the security of your income. If you're somebody who's got guaranteed income such as pensions, things of that nature, you may be able to get away with the three months depending on your comfort and expenses.

But for someone whose entire income depends on a job. Well, that job loss means no more income- so you'd be better off at six. Now, here's the reality again. For most people who are starting off on their financial independence journey, that's unrealistic;

especially with debt. No worries if that's your situation, I'd say at bare minimum you'd want to have a thousand dollars in savings. That's going to cover your typical car repairs, emergency plane ticket, medical expenses etc. With that said, I challenge you to get a thousand dollars in your savings **as fast as you possibly can.**

You'd be surprised how fast you can do it. What can you sell? What can you cut? What can you provide? What service can you do? What can you create in order to get that thousand dollars in your savings as fast as humanly possible? That's going to give you an immediate fresh breath of security if you don't already have it.

It's also going to allow you to focus on other things that must happen in order for you to begin building wealth such as paying down debt. So get your bare minimum thousand dollars in savings as fast as humanly possible. Once you do, then you can start to focus on debt.

I recommend keeping it separate from your normal bank account, maybe even at a different bank. Why? Because, if you're just starting out, then in most cases, you'll be tempted to touch it. But hey, you know yourself. I tend to subscribe to the out of sight, out of mind ideology. If I see it when I log into my normal banking app, I'm more tempted to tap into it. You know how your brain will justify doing what your higher self really knows you shouldn't? Why put yourself in that situation?

Look for high yield savings accounts, money markets, or even no penalty CDs. These are all different places to hold your emergency fund. You want to look for the highest interest rate that you can find while still keeping the money liquid and accessible. But just know that you're not going to make a whole lot of interest on that money, and that's ok. It's really not there for interest. It's there for security.

Another tip for protecting your emergency fund, especially for those in relationships, is to predetermine what qualifies in your book as an emergency beforehand. You might not deem something as an emergency, that your significant other does. So get on the same page, beforehand.

Congrats! You've planned out your dollars; you're prioritizing how you spend, and you've built the emergency fund. Time to tackle the debt.

DEALING WITH DEBT

I'll spare you the statistics. This whole country operates in debt, visit www.usdebtclock.org and see for yourself! So it's no surprise Americans have massive debt as well. The bottom line is, you can't build true wealth, while still in debt. There is such a thing as good debt and bad debt. Good debt helps you make money. For instance, using a line of credit to invest in an appreciating asset. Bad debt only costs you money in interest. For this chapter we're focused on the bad. So, let's first talk about the types of debt, and what you need to do to get rid of them.

Types of Debt

There are two types: *secured* and *unsecured.* Secured debt is when property or assets that have enough value are pledged as collateral to cover the debt. The agreement is created with what's called a *lien*. If you default on the payments, the property will likely be sold to repay the debt. The biggest type of secured debt that most are familiar with is a mortgage. Typically, with secured debt, you will have lower interest rates. But it also comes with the threat of foreclosure, or repossession in the case of vehicles, if you default.

Unsecured debt does not require collateral. The debtor's credit profile is reviewed to determine worthiness and ability to repay the debt before making the decision to lend the money. With unsecured debt you'll typically have higher interest rates and your credit history will come into factor much more.

I recommend eliminating as much of your debt as possible before purchasing a home. That's for many obvious reasons, but also because it will allow you to qualify for the best mortgage due to a low debt to income ratio (DTI).

Your debt to income ratio determines the percentage of your income that's used to pay your debt. Mortgage lenders assess your ability to manage monthly payments and qualify for a mortgage largely based on your debt-to-income ratio. They consider both your front, and back-end DTI. Front-end is the percentage that strictly covers all mortgage costs including your principal, interest, taxes, insurance, and HOA fees. 36% or less is ideal.

Your backend DTI, includes *all* debt, including any child support or alimony. 43% or less is ideal. So ultimately your ideal DTI is 36/43. With land and real estate being some of the greatest assets you can own, you want to position yourself as low as possible with these numbers for the greatest mortgage possible.

Paying Down Debt

The two, most common strategies for paying down debt are the debt snowball, and the debt avalanche. There is also a third, lesser known strategy that I'll share as well. Here's how the first two work.

With the debt snowball, take all of your debt and list it out from the smallest balance to largest balance. Now, you're going to put the biggest payment that you can on the lowest balance, and only pay the minimum payments on all the others. The idea here is that the more money you put towards that lowest balance, the faster you pay it off.

Once it's paid off move on to the next, again taking all the money you can, which should be larger now that the first is gone, and apply it to the next lowest balance. In this way, you build momentum to keep going until all the debt is paid.

With the debt avalanche, you're going to start again by listing out all of your debt; only this time, you're going to line them up by interest rate. You're going to put the biggest payment on the highest interest rate, and pay the minimum payments on all the others. You may not pay the debt off as quickly as with the snowball because you're not focused on the lowest balance, you're focused on the highest interest rate. Why do it this way? The motivation here is the savings that you will experience by paying off the balance with the highest interest rate more quickly. Since this can take longer you really want to make sure you're disciplined in sticking to your payments. Most people opt for the snowball because you can see the wins more quickly than with the avalanche.

A lesser known, third strategy focuses on paying whichever debt will have the biggest impact on increasing your cash flow. By calculating what's called the Cash Flow Index (CFI), you can determine which debt to go after first. Simply divide your balance by your minimum payment to find the CFI. For example, a credit card with a $7000 balance and a $150 monthly payment has a Cash Flow Index of 46.6. Find the CFI for each of your debts and aggressively go after the lowest ones first, especially those with a CFI under 50. These will create the most significant increase to your cash flow as opposed to the debt snowball or avalanche.

When beginning to go after your debt with any of these strategies another simple, but often overlooked thing you can do is to just reach out to your creditors and ask for lower interest rates. You'd be surprised at how a simple phone conversation with the right person can create such a huge impact. Try negotiating your rates- especially if you've got a solid payment history, or length of time as a customer etc. Essentially any leverage you can use, go for it and don't be afraid to ask.

If it doesn't work, then using some debt consolidation strategies can be very helpful in paying off your debt more quickly than paying multiple individual debts. Here are a few ways to consolidate.

0% Percent Interest Credit Cards

Taking a balance that's on a 10% interest card and putting it on a 0% interest card will help you tremendously. Be mindful of transfer fees.

Home Equity Lines of Credit (H.E.L.O.C.)

If you're a homeowner and have equity built up in your home, you can take out a home equity line of credit in order to pay off your debts. Now all debts except your HELOC read as a zero balance. Typically these lines of credit have lower interest rates since they are secured by the home. Be mindful that taking out a HELOC does have closing costs associated with creating the line of credit. This can be a good strategy if you plan to sell the home in the near future as well since the sale will clear the debt altogether.

Retirement Plan Loans

Similar to the HELOC or the zero percent interest credit cards, it is possible to take a loan from your 401(k) or 403(b) etc., pay off all of your debt; and then pay yourself back over time. The process is usually very quick, and flexible in terms of when and how long you pay back the money. Again, you'll typically have lower interest on these loans. In most cases you can take a loan of up to a certain percentage of the balance within your retirement plan, with a limit of usually $50k. The thing to be mindful of here is your job security. Even if you lose your job, you're still required to pay that loan. If you default on the payments, then the outstanding balance becomes considered as income for the year, and therefore taxable. This may or may not be the biggest of deals, but worth considering. It's also worth noting that when you do this, you are taking money out of the market where it has growth potential so be very mindful of doing so, and consider your other options first.

Cash Value Loans from Life Insurance

For those that have permanent life insurance policies with built up cash value, you can take a loan from that cash value in order to pay off all your debts. Similar to the retirement plan loans, if you default on the loan, the outstanding balance becomes taxable income for the year, and you are also diminishing the growth potential of those funds by taking them out of the market.

BANKRUPTCY

Debt elimination through bankruptcy is a viable, but last resort; and there are two very common types for individuals.

Chapter 7 Bankruptcy

Filing for a Chapter 7 bankruptcy is a way of getting out from under many types of debt that you can no longer afford the monthly payments for. As soon as you file, a court order stops creditors from taking any collection actions, such as repossession, against you. From there the court takes legal possession of your property, and a court-appointed trustee is assigned to begin liquidating your nonexempt assets to pay the creditors. This is why it is typically called a liquidation bankruptcy.

Certain factors, including the value of your assets, determine what does and does not get sold. Things like your home, your vehicle, and many other items are often exempt. It's not uncommon to have your debt wiped clean without having to sell much. This is a common misconception about Chapter 7, that you'll need to sell everything, which more often than not, just isn't the case.

The bankruptcy will stay on your credit for ten years after the date you file, which will impact you being able to qualify for other things like a mortgage. Typically, but not always, you will not be eligible for a new mortgage until two years after the discharge of the bankruptcy.

Eligibility for Chapter 7 is determined based on if your income is lower than the median income for the same sized household in your state. If not, then Chapter 13 is likely your next option.

Chapter 13 Bankruptcy

Chapter 13 is different in that your debts are not totally wiped clean. The bankruptcy court deems that you do make enough money to pay back some or all of your debts over a three-to-five year period through a repayment plan. It's for this reason that Chapter 13's are called Wage Earner's Plans. Within that repayment plan they are consolidating and prioritizing your debt. Things like alimony, child support and unpaid taxes are given top priority and must be paid in full. If you are behind on your mortgage or auto loan, the arrears must be paid through the repayment plan in order to retain the home or car, possibly at a lower interest rate. Unsecured debts such as credit cards or medical debt are considered low priority and paid a minimal amount if anything within the plan; oftentimes erased, just depending on your case.

Payments for your bankruptcy are paid either from payroll deductions or directly from your bank account. During the bankruptcy, you are not able to incur new debt such as a mortgage etc. without consulting the trustee first since the new debt payments may compromise your ability to make your payments. If you fail to make payments, the court may either convert your bankruptcy to a chapter 7, or dismiss your case altogether.

Be mindful, there are administrative court fees as well as trustee fees built into the repayment plan that do take priority before the debts.

Because you are paying down some of your debts rather than wiping them clean, a Chapter 13 will stay on your credit for 7 years from the date you file, rather than 10 years.

Make no mistake, being in Chapter 13 is tough, but not impossible. If you are having trouble paying all of your different monthly payments, consolidating them into one payment, oftentimes at a lower interest rate is much more manageable. It is still very possible to have a quality and enjoyable life; however, you will need to learn to plan and prioritize your spending very quickly to make it work. Don't be surprised if you find yourself needing to generate extra income from a side hustle or business.

There's a very negative stigma around bankruptcy that I, for personal, and fact-based reasons believe needs to be dropped. Bankruptcy can change a person's life. Too often it's looked at as a sign of failure and irresponsibility. I know I personally carried that shame until really reflecting on its value and experiencing its long-term benefits. I say that to say that if you're in that position, go easy on yourself and use the bankruptcy to make you better.

A key thing to remember with either form of bankruptcy is that your retirement accounts are protected from the bankruptcy. This matters because threatening calls and letters from creditors can push those unaware of this law to withdraw funds from their retirement accounts. That means paying taxes, and even potential penalties, all in an effort to pay those debts. Be careful! Withdrawing retirement funds create additional taxes, and if you are under age 59 ½, likely also means penalties as well. Every situation is different, but it's usually best to save the taxes and penalties and file for bankruptcy if that's what you need to do.

At the end of the day, it's important to be mindful that as long as you carry debt, you are paying someone else instead of paying yourself and building wealth. When talking about wealth- it's not about what you make, it's about what you keep.

SUMMARY

Let's recap. First and foremost, we've worked to begin or continue shifting our mindset around money by identifying our core beliefs and money scripts as well as releasing any financial trauma. We've developed an overall vision for ourselves and laid out goals to get there. We know our whys and have our affirmations to keep us both grounded and focused along the way.

Now you've put yourself on a simplified monthly or annual "B" word, which we know as a plan for our dollars. You're practicing your prioritization in order to help you stick to the plan while paying down your debt in a strategic way. Remember, your emergency fund of at least $1000 is the top priority before going after the debt. Now your cash flow is in order and it's only a matter of time until you're debt free, but in the meantime you should already be feeling much more confident and in control with some clarity around your finances.

From here we want to begin to put some armor on. What I mean is protection from some of the more serious risks of life. An emergency fund is great for the pop up situations, but what about the bigger risks that life can present such as a disability, incapacitation or even death?

CHAPTER III

RISK MANAGEMENT WITH DISABILITY, LONG-TERM CARE & LIFE INSURANCE

I clearly remember one of my clients named James from my days working in the banks. James was a tall and easy-going kind of guy that had made an impression on me because he had built his own successful business as an electrician. He was not too much older than I was; a family man with three kids and a wife. We had a good working relationship. These were the days before everything you needed was on an app, so every few days he'd come in first thing in the morning, grab a cup of coffee and pull up a chair to check his accounts as well as talk with me for a few.

Things went on like that for a few months, then I noticed I hadn't seen James in a few weeks. Soon after, one day he rolled into the bank in a wheelchair. He was moving slower, and his speech was a bit off. He told me he'd been in a car accident; no fault of his own either. It had definitely set him back. Doctors told him his healing process could be anywhere from 8-10 months, which meant he had to shut his business down for a bit while he recovered.

I immediately thought about his family. He asked me to double check to make sure his disability income started direct depositing so I pulled up his account, and sure enough, there it was. Smart move James! I tell this story because it was my first encounter with disability insurance and I'll never forget it.

You'd be shocked to know that American adults are five times more likely to become disabled than die prematurely. But more often than not, we are more financially prepared for death than disability. Let me ask you this- right now, if you were to become disabled, meaning you cannot work, what would that mean for your income? Even further, what would that mean for your household?

This is where disability insurance comes in. Disability insurance provides income in the event. that the policyholder is prevented from earning income due to physical and/ or mental injury or illness.

There's three types of disability insurance: Social Security Disability Income (SSDI), Short term Disability, and Long term Disability.

SOCIAL SECURITY DISABILITY INCOME

The positive about SSDI is that once you begin receiving it, it may last until what's considered your Full Retirement Age (65-67). At that point it would then convert to retirement benefits typically at the same amount. So it's a long term solution. However, it's reviewed frequently based on the recipient's condition to make sure it is still needed, and it is notoriously hard to qualify for.

When applying for SSDI you must first have paid into Social Security in the past either through employment or from your self employment. So for entrepreneurs who have not ever paid into Social Security, you'll need to look elsewhere. But if you've worked at employers in the past, you're good to go. In addition you must have a condition that meets Social Security's very strict definition of disability which does not include partial disability. In other words, SSDI will not pay out if your condition does not severely limit your ability to do even basic work-related activities such as lifting, standing, walking, sitting or even remembering things! In addition this must be for at least 12 months.

The amount the recipient receives is based on their age and work history and there is a monthly maximum that can be received. It is reduced when earned income exceeds a certain limit. So if you're disabled, but still able to generate some income, you want to be mindful of this.

The reduction based on other income also applies if, say for instance, assets are left to you by parents, family etc. to help support you. So if you have a child with disabilities who receives SSDI, and you want to leave assets to them as a part of your estate planning, working with an estate attorney will be crucial. They will most likely advise you to establish what's called a Special Needs Trust. We'll discuss this more in our estate planning chapter. On to the more common types of disability from here.

Short & Long- Term Disability

There is short-term, disability and long-term disability. With short term, the disability income usually can be provided for up to one year.

It's typically going to replace anywhere from 60-70% of the income you were receiving from salary or from your own business, and you can access it through either group coverage, typically through your employer; or, you can go out and purchase a private policy of your own.

With long-term disability, the income can be provided up until the age of retirement, or until you return to work. It's typically going to replace anywhere from 40-70% of your income; and similar to short-term, can be accessed at group rates or through private insurance policies.

What should you be mindful of when choosing your disability? You want to be aware of the actual cost, which is known as, the premium. Premiums are typically very affordable; and that's one of the shocking things about disability, is that 67% of American workers do not have long-term disability, yet 41% of employers offer it. (Source: simplyinsurance.com) So there's a disconnect where we're just simply not taking advantage of it.

The elimination period is also a crucial point. Elimination periods are basically the waiting period before the disability insurance begins payout. So, in other words, this is the period that you must go without any income from the insurance company. Shorter elimination periods are typically 0 to 30 days, whereas longer elimination periods are typically 60-90 days. As you can probably imagine, the shorter the elimination period, the higher the premiums. Being strategic in your situation is key. If you've got the true emergency savings, you may feel comfortable with the longer elimination period, or maybe not, up to you.

Why is there an elimination period in the first place? This is the insurance company's way of "qualifying" you to truly make sure you're disabled. They're looking to avoid a scenario where you're going to recover quickly, but turning the insurance on to bring in some extra income from them.

Premiums and elimination periods are important, but perhaps the biggest of all is understanding what the insurance company defines as "disabled." Will the income begin based on partial, or total disability? Partial disability is when an injury or illness prevents a worker from performing duties of *their* occupation. Whereas total disability is when an injury or illness prevents a worker from performing *any* occupation.

You'll want to be very clear on that verbiage within your policy. If you are partially disabled and unable to perform your specific occupation and you need income, you'd hate to be stuck in a policy that will only pay based on your inability to work at all.

Last is the taxability of the income. You're already receiving 60-70% of the income you were receiving while working. You'd hate for that income to be taxed in addition to already being a reduced amount. So when you pay for your premiums with pretax dollars, in other words dollars that have not been taxed, the disability income will be taxable.

So, for W-2 employees, in most cases your employer pays your disability premiums and receives a tax deduction for those premiums. Be aware that this means your disability income, if ever needed, would be taxable. If you were to purchase an individual policy on your own, you'd be paying with after-tax dollars, which would allow the disability income to be tax free. The same goes for entrepreneurs and business owners. Depending on if you are paying for your own premiums or your employees' premiums, from the business; then your business will be able to deduct those as a business expense. However, if you are paying for your disability from your after-tax income, the disability income you receive would be tax free. The choice is yours.

This sums up the main points on disability insurance. On to long-term care.

Long-Term Care

Thomas and Jean came to me a couple months before he was retiring. They were both in their late 60's with no children. They lived simply and had more money than they would ever spend. After multiple meetings and helping them button up their financial plan for retirement, I noticed Jean handled more of the financial details. I had a phone call with her and she shared with me Thomas' family history of how all the men for the past three generations had dealt with Alzheimers. It was something she wanted to ensure they were prepared for if/ when the time came for Thomas. To do so she had placed a chunk of cash into a CD at her bank. I definitely agreed that it was the biggest threat to their finances. But, what I was able to add that Jean hadn't considered, was the thought of her own care. She was so focused on him that it hadn't dawned on her that if she handled his elder care and he passed before her; with no children, who would care for her in her elder years? After more planning and discussion, I felt it was right for both Jean and Thomas to purchase long-term care policies with some of the cash rather than leaving it in a CD. The best part is, they ended up with much more money for long-term care through the combined total of the policies than what she'd originally put to the side, plus she still had cash left over!

It's a fact of life that as we age not only do our bodies start to decline, but so can our minds. Many of the millennials reading this are in the sandwich of having children, but also managing the care, or potential future care of baby boomer parents. So it is imperative that we understand how caring for the elderly and incapacitated works, especially from a financial perspective.

Seven out of ten Americans who reach the age of 65 will need long-term care at some point in their life, typically by age 80. Let that number sink in: 7 out of 10! What may be even more shocking is that the estimated median monthly price of assisted living in America, by 2030 will be near $6000 per month. If mom needs care, who's going to pay?

Long-term care is prescribed when an individual is unable to perform two of the activities of daily living (ADL's) for a period of at least 90 days. Those include: eating, dressing, bathing, transferring, toileting, and continence. There's also some secondary ADL's called Instrumental ADL's and those are: financial management, shopping, meal prep, housework, medication and transportation.

Most people have one picture in mind when they hear "long-term care," and that's the nursing home; but, there's more to it. Long-term care can be broken down into three levels. There's in-home care, assisted living, then finally nursing home facilities.

With home healthcare it's just as it sounds, an aide comes to the home who can assist with cooking, cleaning, errands as well as the activities of daily living. Most people want to stay in their home for as long as possible so it makes sense that things start off with home health care, and progress from there. The median annual cost for a home health aide in 2021 was $61,800 which has risen 12.5% from 2020.

Adult day care centers offer a community setting with planned activities and are supervised by caregivers; whereas assisted living facilities offer personal care and health services in a residential setting. Assisted living comes out less expensive than the personal touch of a home health aide coming in at $54k median annual cost in 2021.

Last is the nursing facility. Mental illnesses such as Alzheimer's and Dementia, Stroke, Diabetes, Parkinson's disease or Multiple Sclerosis are some of the leading causes of patients requiring long term care within a nursing home. Caregivers provide assistance with the activities of daily living, medication, therapy, rehabilitation and more. Nursing home facilities offer both private and shared rooms at different price points and the state makes a big difference as well. For instance, the median annual cost for a private room in Louisiana in 2021 was approx. $64k; whereas in New York it was close to $160k

How do you pay for long-term care? There's three main approaches: Out of pocket, Government Assistance and Long-term Care Insurance.

Self-insuring or paying out of your own pocket for long-term care will obviously provide the most flexibility and control.

However, as we've seen, the costs can be significant. While I've seen many who, either can, or do approach long term care in this way; I caution my clients to consider these factors. First are taxes. If assets need to be liquidated, there are likely to be taxes on the gains those assets have experienced over time prior to being sold. If the assets being sold are held within retirement accounts, the taxes are even greater since every penny is considered income and therefore taxed at ordinary income tax rates. So, even if you have the assets to cover the costs, why cause yourself excess taxes? Also, your out-of-pocket will likely be greater than the cost of the insurance premiums. So again, why cause yourself excess costs rather than leveraging other people's money through insurance while saving yours?

It's a common misconception that Medicare will cover long term care costs, which is not entirely true. Medicare, which is the federal health care provided to individuals 65 and older, has very limited provisions when long-term care is required, and it is for very specific situations. It's more of the exception rather than the norm. Medicaid is a federal and state run program providing health coverage to low income households and individuals, and does include long term care costs. There are strict income and asset limits that must be met by the individual needing the care. A quick google search in your desired state will help you find the income and asset limits that apply for your situation. Overall, medicaid is a viable option; however, as you can imagine with government assistance programs, the care may not be up to your standards for you or your loved one(s).

There are two main types of Long-term care insurance. There's the traditional stand- alone policies which have been around the longest, and the newer linked-benefit, or commonly called, hybrid policies. Let's start with the traditional as they're the most simple to understand.

As with any insurance, it's a contract between you, the owner, and the insurance company. You pay a premium, they promise a certain amount of coverage when two ADL's cannot be performed and LTC is prescribed. As long as premiums are paid, you've got coverage. Easy enough right? But there are some knocks on the traditional policy that have made them less popular, the biggest of which is their use it or lose it nature.

I've had clients who saw their parents pay into traditional long-term care policies for 30 plus years. That's a long time to pay for something you're not guaranteed to use right? What happens if you're the 85 year old still going strong, or just never need the policy? All that money, for all that time, down the drain.

Traditional long-term care policies are still a viable option, because they are, in the short term, significantly less expensive than hybrid policies. However, they are not as dynamic as the linked- benefit policies of today because of their ongoing payments, and use it or lose it structure.

When considering a traditional policy, some solid guidelines and considerations to evaluate if it's worth it are if the premiums are more than 5% of your monthly income; the inflation rate on the benefits; how many ADL's are required to begin payout; the elimination period; and obviously, the total benefit and monthly maximum payout. We'll break down all of these in the following section as we discuss hybrid policies.

If you don't remember anything with a hybrid, long-term care policy, remember this: *live, quit* or *die*. Those are the options.

If you live to need the care; it's there for you to "turn on the faucet," so to speak. If you decide you want to quit the policy, you have the option to receive either some, or all of your money back, depending on your policy selection. Finally, when you pass, your family would receive a death benefit similar to a life insurance policy. It sounds almost too good to be true, so let's break this down.

Hybrid long-term care policies are a combination of permanent life and long-term care insurance, thus the linked-benefit. You essentially put cash into the policy via either lump sum, or over a certain amount of time. That's another key difference is that with hybrid, the premiums last for a finite amount of time. Typically anywhere between five to ten years if not paid lump sum.

Based on your total premiums, gender, health, age and many other factors- two amounts are determined. Your total LTC benefit, which is the full amount that the insurance will pay towards your care; and your monthly maximum, or, how much they will pay per month from the total benefit. Both numbers are important, but I do stress the monthly maximum since that's how the funds are paid out. A $450k total benefit is great; but if only $2k is being paid per month, you're coming out of pocket more to supplement the $2k. Versus, maybe a $425k total benefit with a $3500 monthly max. Every situation is different, so this is just general guidance. But be sure to consider them both rather than focusing only on the total benefit, which is easy to do since it's the bigger number.

Once paid, via either lump sum, annually, semi-annually etc.; the cost of the insurance is taken from your premiums, and the rest is considered your cash value. The cash value is what's paid back to you as a return of your premiums should you decide to quit the policy. Companies may or may not have a minimum time period required in the policy before you can surrender it. This goes to show that you'll want to consider these policies as a long-term investment. Before purchasing a policy, there may be an option of choosing how much you would receive if you decided to cancel the policy down the line. Those options would be to either receive the full amount of your premiums paid, or a reduced amount. Choosing a reduced amount would produce a higher benefit, whereas choosing to receive all of your premiums would mean a lower benefit. The choice comes down to what you care about most, the coverage, or the security of being able to cancel.

Now that you have a basic understanding of the functionality of the policy, let's break down its elements individually.

Premium

Again, this is the amount you pay into the policy. It is not necessarily the cost of the insurance itself, but simply the amount you are required to pay. Premiums can be paid annually, semi-annually, quarterly, or monthly. Your premium schedule may be as short as a lump sum, or spread over as many as five to fifteen years.

Cash & Surrender Values

Once you have paid your premium, that year's cost of insurance is deducted and the rest is considered cash value. Depending on your policy, this cash value may be equal, or greater, than what's called your *surrender value*. Your surrender value is the amount you'd receive if you decided to cancel the policy. Again, based on that individual policy's structure, there may or may not be a vesting schedule as to how much you'd receive if you surrender. For instance, a fifteen year vesting schedule means that you'd receive a reduced amount, which would gradually increase to the full cash value, until year fifteen and beyond. The potential advantage of selecting this type of policy is it likely provides a greater total LTC benefit and monthly maximum versus one that would allow for a full return of premium right off the bat. Each company and the policies they offer may differ.

Total LTC Benefit & Monthly Maximum

The LTC benefit is the full amount of money that would ultimately be paid out towards long term care costs before the policy is exhausted. The monthly maximum is how much of that total benefit that would be paid out monthly. As I shared in the example earlier, a total benefit of a large number is great; however, the monthly maximum in my opinion is more impactful because Long-term care expenses are, in most cases, paid monthly. So if your monthly maximum doesn't cover those expenses, you would still need to come out of pocket. There is a page within most long term care policy illustrations where different combinations of LTC benefit and monthly maximums are listed for you to choose from. The numbers are calculated based on the premiums you've decided to pay. For example: A $40,000 premium spread over a 10 year schedule may produce $150,000 of total benefit with a monthly maximum of $1500 as an option to choose from. Another option for that same premium schedule could be $130,000 total benefit with a monthly maximum of $2000. These are simplified numbers just to illustrate that it's the same amount of premium, paid over the same amount of time- just producing different results for you to choose from.

These are the numbers you're doing it all for, so the important thing to remember with these is that it's very unlikely you're going to get a policy that will cover 100% of your long term care costs. Not unless you're ready to invest a very large amount of cash! Instead, you're looking to reduce your potential out of pocket costs. How much should you be looking for? There's no magic number, but you'll want to consider your expected income level in retirement, and how much of that monthly income you want going toward supplementing your insurance.

Inflation Benefit

Because the cost of care continues to rise, your total long term care benefit and monthly maximum need to as well. To accomplish this, at the time of purchase an inflation benefit must be selected. The options are usually 3% or 5%, and whether the rate is simple or compound.

Obviously 5% compound will provide the greatest growth, but it comes at a price. The cost of the insurance will be higher, and ultimately affect all other numbers within the policy. To help make your choice easier, most policies have a page towards the back illustrating how the different rate options impact the monthly maximum and total benefit, based on your premium. Inflation benefits are extremely valuable and come with just about any long term care policy.

Guarantee

Another key thing to consider is the guarantee of the policy. Long-term care insurance providers have really taken a hit due to the inflation in that industry. So when you purchase an insurance policy, and this goes for any life insurance as well, you want to make sure that the company is very financially sound in order to be able to pay those claims when they arise.

A great feature to have in hybrid long-term care policies is a day one guarantee of your total benefit and monthly max. The guarantee applies the minute you pay your first premium, even if you're scheduled for 10 years of premiums. So if for any reason you needed care in the very first year of having the policy, those benefits are locked in and will begin paying out. Of course, if that were to happen, your benefit would not have experienced much inflation; however, it's a great security blanket to have. Guarantees are a sign of a financially sound insurance company.

Benefit Duration Period

No one knows if and/ or when they will need long term care. Nor do they know for how long. Still, when purchasing a policy, you'll need to decide on the benefit duration period. These periods can range from one year to as long as you live. Those are rare and typically apply to the government and military. The common range is usually about 3-7 years. The average LTC claim beginning from home health care to nursing facility is between 5-6 years and begins at age 80. However, with life expectancies getting longer and technological advances in healthcare, this is changing. The majority of clients I've worked with choose around 5-6 years of benefit duration. Meaning that if there's a total benefit of $400k, it will pay out over that time and end when the time's up.

Death Benefit

Because the policy is a hybrid between life and long term care insurance, there is a tax free death benefit paid to your beneficiary(ies) should you pass without using the care. The death benefit is usually the value of the premiums plus an additional 10-20%. This additional 10-20% typically still pays out even if the care is used because of the policy's life insurance component.

Elimination Period

As with disability insurance, long term care policies have elimination periods. In the long term care world, it's typically 90 days. Once the elimination period is met beginning in month four, the policy will pay the first three months' in addition to the payment of the fourth.

Indemnity vs. Reimbursement

You'll want to be certain whether the plan is an indemnity or reimbursement plan as they pay out very differently. With reimbursement, the policy is reimbursing the costs of care for that month. Receipts, bills etc. are required for qualifying expenses to justify the payout to either you or a facility. The exact amount of the cost of care for that month, up to the maximum, is reimbursed.

With indemnity plans, once you are qualified as needing long term care, you are able to request up to the monthly maximum each month to spend as you please. There are no requirements for bills and receipts etc. For those who choose to have a family member care for them, this allows the owner of the policy to pay the family member, rather than needing proof of care from a facility etc.

Indemnity provides a lot more flexibility.

OTHER WAYS TO PAY FOR LONG-TERM CARE

Life Insurance

You can also use a life insurance policy that has either what are called living benefits, or specifically has what's called a long-term care rider. A rider is nothing more than an added feature on top of a life insurance policy.

With either living benefits or long-term care riders, if long term care is needed, the policy will begin to pay an accelerated death benefit to the owner to help cover those costs. For instance, if you have a $500,000 life insurance policy, and you need long-term care; with this rider, that $500,000 which normally would've gone to your family upon your death, will begin paying to you.

The pro is that these will be less expensive than hybrid long-term care policies; but the con is the lack of an inflation benefit. So consider that when making your decisions. Keep in mind though, something is better than nothing, and while they're not specifically LTC policies, they are a swiss army knife of coverage, giving you multiple protections in one. A word of advice with all of these policies whether life, disability or LTC is to give special attention to who the insurance carrier will allow to determine whether you're able to perform ADL's. You'd much rather it be allowable for your doctor to determine the need, than having to be approved by a doctor appointed by the insurance carrier.

Home Equity

Utilizing equity within a home whether through a home equity line of credit, home equity loan or reverse mortgage. With the first two, repayment must begin once you've tapped the equity, and also require good credit and proof of income. However, a reverse mortgage is unique. A reverse mortgage allows homeowners who are 62 and older to convert the equity in their homes into cash to pay for long-term care. The lender is essentially loaning you money for the value of your home, while you get to stay in it and hold the title. The payments of that equity are tax-free and can be issued via either lump sum, a credit line, monthly or a combination of all three. They do not affect your social security, SSDI or medicare as they are not considered income; however, it can affect medicaid which is a needs- based program..

They work best for those who are intending to stay in their home at least three years or have one spouse in a facility while the other is home. The repayment to the lender comes due as soon as the last homeowner either sells the house, moves, passes away or becomes delinquent on property taxes and insurance. Allowing the home to go into disrepair can also cause repayment to come due. At that time, the lender will sell the home to recoup any money paid out, with any remaining equity going to your heirs. Be clear this is not a strategy for the coveted generational wealth. Why? Because the house is not being left to the kids or family. Reverse mortgages are very complex, and there are scams out there. Doing your due diligence is definitely advised.

Long term care is something we can't ignore. Hopefully this overview has given you a starting place to evaluate your plan. Let's move onto the last of the insurances covered in this book, life insurance.

LIFE INSURANCE

The power of life insurance cannot be understated; especially in underserved communities. Stagnation, struggle and even poverty will perpetuate without it. However, with life insurance, the power to transform the future of not only our individual families, but our communities and even cultures exists. Life insurance, besides real estate, is the single most powerful tool for establishing, conserving, and continuing sustainable wealth.

Nine times out of ten for the average household, the whole point of having the policy is for its death benefit. This is the amount paid to your heirs upon your death. A death benefit is **tax free**. Think about that for a minute. A tax free, lump sum paid to those you love when you pass. What can that do for your spouse, or your children?

There's been a longstanding common misconception that life insurance was only meant for burial expenses; and that it was too expensive to have. Because of these misconceptions, many families are missing out on significant income replacement in the event of a spouse, or breadwinner passing away prematurely. Beyond income replacement the ability to establish wealth for generational advancement is also severely impacted because of the misconception.

The baby boomer generation will transfer over $50 trillion dollars of wealth over the next 20 years. The wealth gap will only get wider if the middle and lower class does not take advantage of the tools available- life insurance being one of the biggest ones. So let's get into the two types.

Term & Permanent

There's term, or temporary, life insurance; and there's permanent as well. With temporary insurance, the goal is to secure your income in case you pass away before retiring. Ideally, the death benefit would allow your spouse to pay off the mortgage etc; send the kids to college; live comfortably for some time, or maybe even go back to school if needed to reenter the workforce; you get the picture. Again, because it's temporary, you choose the term. Term policies can range from 5-30 years.

How do you determine how much you need? There's different ways with varying degrees of depth in the calculation when doing so. The most basic way is to multiply your annual income by ten, then add any college expenses for your children. Another simple, yet more in depth way of determining how much life insurance coverage you'd need is by using the acronym L.I.F.E.; which stands for *Liabilities, Income, Funeral* (or Family), and *Education* (or Everything else).

Liabilities are straightforward. Include the mortgage and any other debt you'd want paid.

For income, consider these points. First, how much annual income are you needing to replace? Is it 100% of what you were bringing in; more, or depending on your situation, maybe less. Next would be, for how long? Is it until you'd retire, or a lesser period of time until your spouse could adjust? Only you and your spouse can determine that based on your situation. Finally, consider inflation. Whatever that amount needed is now, is not the same 5 years from now, or even 3 years from now. Factor in inflation. You can easily do this with a life insurance calculator online. One final tip here is that your spouse would need to reinvest life insurance proceeds to keep pace with future inflation once they receive the money. This is of course, after their emergency fund and whatever necessary expenses are paid. All that excess cash sitting in a bank is no good, because it will lose its purchasing power to the natural rise in the cost of living as time goes by.

Funeral, and/ or family expenses are also straightforward. If there's individual circumstances with your family that require funding, consider them here.

Education expenses can be costly. Determine the in-state or out-of-state tuition costs for the kids; and look at what your spouse may need education-wise if that's a factor as well. But don't forget the inflation. Of course, anything else, throw it in. Again, using a life insurance calculator that factors in inflation can make this a simple task. I like Edward Jones' here

Now you've got a ballpark figure of how much insurance coverage you need. Where do you go to get it?

Employers are going to offer term insurance in most cases. It's annually renewable through your benefits enrollment period, and the coverage amount is typically based on your salary. In most cases you may be able to access 5-6x your salary in insurance coverage. Again a common misconception is that this is going to be enough. Hopefully by now, you've seen it's not.

I strongly encourage you to look outside of your employer for the coverage you need for a few reasons:

The first being that if you lose your job for any reason, that insurance does not go with you, unless you pay for it out of pocket. Anything connected with your employer potentially ceases when you separate from them.

Second is that, unless you are 35 or younger, you will likely find better insurance rates on your own; and you will be able to access the coverage you need rather than being capped at a certain multiple of your salary. I'm not saying don't take advantage of the employer offer, just don't stop there.

Another huge reason to look outside of your employer is for living benefits on your policy. Living benefits will provide an accelerated death benefit in the event of certain illnesses. These include critical illnesses such as heart attacks, stroke, some cancers and more. Chronic illness, also considered LTC (Long-term care), is covered. And terminal illness is covered as well. Living benefits often extend to even critical injuries such as severe burns, brain trauma and more. Depending on the insurance carrier, these living benefits can come standard with the policy; but that's typically not the case with one from your employer.

One final reason to seek coverage outside of your employer is for convertibility into permanent insurance. Which we'll talk about more below; however, one final note on life insurance through your employer- if you are having health challenges and are unable to get coverage elsewhere, then group insurance can be a great option for guaranteed coverage.

Term insurance will always be less expensive than permanent since it's not guaranteed that the insurance company will need to cut a check. During what's called the *underwriting* process, your age, health, medical history etc. are all reviewed in order to determine the terms and overall approval of the policy. However, the younger you are, generally speaking, the less expensive it will be since you are statistically less likely to pass.

Permanent life insurance operates differently and is built on different goals. With permanent insurance, as long as the premiums are paid, or there is cash within the policy to support the cost of the insurance, the insurance company is on the hook to cut a check regardless of when you pass, even if you live to 120! It comes in the form of either what's called *whole life* insurance, or *universal life* insurance. So while it can serve as income replacement for your loved ones should you pass- typically the intention is aimed towards either funeral expenses for the elderly (via small whole life policies often called final expense or burial insurance), or legacy and wealth transfer. Because of its permanency, these policies are going to be more expensive than term, so achieving the same coverage level as term is usually not feasible for most budgets. But again, this death benefit is to serve a different purpose; and so, based on your goals, may or may not need to be the same amount.

There are policies that allow you to do both within one through what's called *convertibility*. It's done by securing a death benefit via term, that allows you to convert a portion at a time over to permanent. For example, a $1.5M term policy that you gradually move to permanent as you progress in your career and income etc. It may be $50k at a time, or you can choose to do more, it's up to you. But having the flexibility is a great option to achieve both goals.

There are some nuances with permanent policies worth discussing, so let's get into them.

First is the cash value. As with the hybrid long term care, your premiums are not the same as the actual cost of the insurance. When premiums are paid, the cost of the insurance is debited, and the remainder is called cash value. This cash value gives you some options. Within what are called Variable Universal Life policies (VULs), the premiums are flexible and the cash value can be invested in the market as you choose. Within Universal Life policies (ULs), the premiums are again flexible and the cash value will earn an interest rate determined by current market rates, but never below a guaranteed minimum. With Indexed Universal Life policies (IULs), premiums are also flexible, and the cash value, while not directly invested in the stock market, will mirror the performance of a stock index such as the S&P 500. Finally, with Whole life policies, the premiums are fixed and cash value will grow at a guaranteed fixed rate determined by the insurer.

Cash value grows tax deferred, which is a nice benefit to have, and can either be borrowed against or withdrawn from. Withdrawals create income taxes on whatever portion is growth beyond the principal amount. For example, if you're invested cash value was $20k, and it grew to $30k; when you withdraw $5k for that summer cruise, it's coming last-in-first-out (LIFO). Meaning it's coming from the growth, which hasn't been taxed; and therefore, you will pay ordinary income tax on it that year. A loan however does not create tax, unless you default on paying the loan to yourself back. When taking a loan, there is an interest rate applied by the insurer.

I've seen many real estate investors with cash value policies use this as a strategy to move quickly on investment property down payments etc. rather than waiting on loan approvals from banks. This can also be a nice way for entrepreneurs to access funding for themselves in a pinch. Finally, there are retirement income strategies built around the capabilities of such policies where during the working years a policy owner will overfund the policy and allow the cash value to grow tax deferred, all for the goal of pulling out the cash via policy loans as an additional tax free income stream in retirement. This is called a L.I.R.P. strategy, or Life Insurance Retirement Plan strategy and can be very advantageous for high income earners wanting to save more for retirement than what traditional retirement account limits allow. Entrepreneurs often view this as a way of saving for retirement while gaining some coverage at the same time. It has also been called Infinity Banking, and has become popular on social media; however, often misrepresented. I highly recommend working with not only a licensed, but experienced insurance agent since you'll not only want to get the correct policy, but also review it consistently.

Permanent policies can be paid on indefinitely, or they can be "paid up;" which means there's enough cash value in the policy to support the ongoing costs without you having to pay any more premiums. But do remember, there is a cost to that insurance each year regardless of if you are still paying premiums or not. You can structure when that policy is paid up on the front end by working with your insurance rep; but, an annual review of your policy with either your financial planner or rep is a good idea to ensure that the cash value is on pace to support the rising cost of the insurance as you age.

One other wrinkle to permanent policies is the ability for them to be established as survivorship policies. This basically means owned by, and insuring two individuals rather than one; making it essentially a joint policy. This is beneficial to lower the premiums. Think about it, if two people have to pass rather than one, that's typically going to take longer, allowing the insurance company more time before they'll need to write a check. Voila! Lower price.

There you have it, these are the ins and outs of both term and permanent life insurance as well as the goals behind them both. They each serve purposes. If you are early in your career, leaning more toward term is not a bad idea. Just be mindful that there's a very low percentage of term policies that end up being paid out. That means money down the drain so to speak. You need to have some life insurance even if you are single with no kids. Should you have permanent insurance? Maybe, maybe not. But, for the sake of keeping the door open to the future, having a policy that can convert over time is a great option.

How much should you pay for your life insurance? A general guideline as to how much you should pay is at least 6% of your gross income, plus 1% for each dependent. Other factors play into this as well, but it's a nice generalized rule of thumb.

As with long term care, or any insurance, life insurance is a legally binding contract. This is important and provides you with security in knowing that your insurance costs cannot easily be increased whenever a company decides. A rate increase must be approved at the state level, since insurance is regulated by the state.

When shopping, you'll want to consider the financial strength and stability of the company. You can do this by looking up the company's independent agency rating. Agencies such as Standard & Poor's, A.M Best, Moody's or Fitch are among the biggest rating agencies. They each have their own grading scale, so what is a great rating for one (Ex. AAA) may only be a good rating at another.

Also evaluate the company on their customer service. Remember, if your family needs to cash in the policy, they're going through a tough time. The last thing you want is for them to get the runaround and bad service.

Life insurance is a key piece of any estate plan, which we will discuss much deeper in chapter seven, so be sure to name your beneficiaries when taking out a policy.

Summary

We covered a ton in this chapter, so let's recap where we are in our blueprint to financial security. First is the mindset. No lasting changes are made until the work's been done there. Then comes the cash management. Within that management are your debt elimination plan and insurance. Again typically your employer will provide some level of disability coverage and even life insurance. But it's never a bad idea to have your own. I understand tight money plans and how it can be challenging to squeeze in insurance, but without it- you're exposed. Some protection is better than none and a great place to look for multiple protections in one are term life insurance policies with living benefits. Now that your mindset is solid, your cash management is flowing, you're actively paying down debt or even debt free (Congrats!) and have some protection in place- we can talk about growth. Let's get into investing.

CHAPTER IV

INVESTING YOUR DOLLARS FOR THE FUTURE YOU

There was nothing special about this guy sitting across the table from me. I don't mean that in a negative way. I'm simply saying that to show you there's no big secret or hidden capability. John's $3M net worth came mostly from his Investments, and partly from his home that was paid off since he and his wife had lived in it for so long. He was in his early 70s. As we sat across my desk from each other, he told me about his life as I pulled up his accounts on my computer. I noticed how long he had owned some Coca-Cola stock. He told me that while his father was working back in the early 50's he'd consistently bought a few shares of Coca-Cola stock and that when his father passed, he inherited it with his siblings.

He went on to tell me how he'd done the same with his own money, and that he'd be passing it down to his kids. Why am I telling you that story? It's simply to show you the power of investing. Especially when combined with time.

Nothing special.

WHAT IS INVESTING?

Investing is a process of purchasing financial instruments that hold value and can be traded all in an effort to generate a positive return over time. Now when you're investing, there's a couple of things that you have to be mindful of. First is what's called your *time horizon*.

In other words, how soon will you need the money? If it's short term such as 1-5 years, do not invest the money. Because when you invest there is a risk of loss. You want to be able to give that money time. It's about the long game. It doesn't have to be as long as John from my example, but long enough to give your money a real shot at growth.

There's a known mathematical rule in the investment world called the Rule of 72. Here's how it works:

However many years you'd like for it to take in order for your money to double, divide 72 by that number. It'll show you what percentage your money needs to grow each year to achieve that. For example, If you want your money to double in 10 years, you need an annual rate of return no less than 7.2% (72 ÷ 10 = 7.2).

What I'm showing you is that you need to set your expectations properly, and don't think this is overnight. There are some great stories of stocks doing crazy numbers in short amounts of times, but real wealth is built over time and with consistency.

Also, with investing- risk and reward (or return) go hand in hand. Typically, your lower risk investments are going to produce lower returns and vice versa. If someone's telling you,

you can take no risk and get a ton of reward, it's probably too good to be true.

You must also know that different investments produce different *types* of returns. For instance, stocks are going to produce gains and possible dividends, which we'll talk more about. Bonds primarily yield interest and some growth in value.

Before we get deeper into why we should invest, let's talk about the myths and the misconceptions.

Oftentimes, we think investing is only for wealthy people. Not true, I teach kids and teenagers how to get started with as little as one dollar.

Another one, is that investing is too risky, and yes, there is risk involved with investing. But if you look at the stock market, It's actually performed at an average of almost 10% over the last 50 years. If you look at 100 years, it's about the same. Side note, remember the law of 72 and how only 7.2% per year would double your money in 10 years? You don't need to be a math genius to be excited right now!

How about the misconception that investing is too complicated? Well, using index funds can simplify the process significantly. We'll talk about those in just a bit. Opening an investment account is as simple as downloading and logging into an app. And buying investments is as easy as buying something off of Amazon.

Finally, underserved communities for many years tended to think that investing was only for one demographic. This misconception is changing, but still holds true for a large majority. That couldn't be farther from the truth. The market is open to anybody and only cares about one color- green.

WHY INVEST?

Besides the ability to build wealth, we need to invest because of inflation. Inflation is the rise in the cost of goods and services over time. And if you look over history, Inflation typically is about 2.5 -3% percent year over year. In other words, things get about two and a half percent more expensive than they were the year before.

If you look at a chart of inflation over the last 100 years you will see that it's up and down, all over the place. There have been more severe spikes of inflation, most recently, since COVID. Inflation hadn't been that high since the late 70s to mid 80s.

What anyone who's experienced high inflation will tell you is that without some way of either making or growing your money, it's getting less powerful and not stretching as far as it used to. To add on to this, the interest rates being earned from banks are nowhere near what they once were.

In the early 1980s. You could get almost 20 percent in interest from a savings account. Think about how risky a savings account is? Outside of inflation, there is none. Good luck getting that today! I have my students look up what the typical major bank is paying in interest. Even on a million dollars held inside a savings account, the interest is often less than two percent.

So what we're saying here is that because of inflation our money needs to keep up, but banks aren't cutting it. So you've got to invest.

There are four main ways to invest:

- **Start a business-** There are more millionaires today than ever before and the majority of them are entrepreneurs/ business owners.

- **Buying a business,** which we'll be focusing on in this book.

- **Real estate**

- **Precious metals** mainly like gold, or commodities such as oil. This is considered old school in today's fast paced world.

Let's focus on buying a business. One of the most common ways to do so is through the stock market which we'll talk about as one type of investment below.

Types of Investments

By far, the two most common investments outside of real estate are stocks and bonds. We'll discuss these and how they work, as well as a few others below.

Stocks

These are pieces of a company that are valued at a price.

Imagine a huge pie sliced into a million pieces. Let's name it Amazon, or Nike, just about whatever company you want to name. Better yet, we'll go with Apple. See what I did there? What if you were able to buy one of those slices for five dollars.

Once you sit it on your plate you'd have three choices: Hold on to it, buy more, or sell it.

If you decided to sell it, the goal would be to sell it for more than what you bought it for. How would that happen? Through the company, making more money.

Stocks create gains and losses through price fluctuations as the company does business, the economy changes, laws and politics change, global environments shift and so much more. They typically act as a gas pedal within your portfolio of assets. In other words, they're primarily there to drive growth in your net worth. That's where you're going to get your growth from.

The S&P (Standard & Poor's) 500, is a market index of the largest 500 publicly traded companies in the United States. An index is a basket of stocks meant to track the performance of a specific section of the economy or market.

Because of its size and diversity the S&P 500 is largely used to represent the entire Equities (stock) market. Some other index examples include the NASDAQ, Dow Jones Industrial Average (DJIA), Russell 3000 etc.

Stocks are classified in many ways. And within many sections. They can be grouped by their size and worth, or in other words, their capitalization. For instance, a large cap worth many multi billions such as Walmart, a mid cap stock worth under $10 billion such as Hasbro, or a small cap stock worth under $2 billion like Krispy Kreme.

Stocks can also be classified by their sector. Is it an energy company? Is it a tech company? Is it in financials or industrials? So on and so forth.

They can be classified by whether they are foreign or domestic, and can even be classified as to how they are typically going to perform. Meaning, are they more geared towards growth, income in the form of dividends, or a combination of the two?

When you purchase individual stock you can purchase what are called the company's common stock shares; or, you could purchase what are called preferred stock shares. These are basically the difference between VIP and regular entry. Preferred shares come with certain benefits like voting rights within the company on certain board issues, or even priority in the line of repayment if the company goes belly up.

That's the jist on stocks and how they work. Let's talk about bonds.

Bonds

Bonds are basically a loan that you've made to a government or company. And they're going to pay you back with interest. It's an IOU that you hold on the issuer of that bond. That IOU can also be sold, and its value can fluctuate in price. Although it's good to know that bond prices don't typically fluctuate like stocks do. This is why they're seen as a safer investment than stocks. If stocks are your gas pedal, bonds are your brake. And just like with any vehicle, when you're on the road, there's a need for both at some point.

Bonds can be classified in many ways as well. Is the issuer a government or corporation? What's their Creditworthiness like? In other words, do they pay their debts? The creditworthiness of issuers is rated by independent agencies to give investors insight into the safety of that investment the same way you have a credit report evaluated by banks etc. This is where the term "junk bonds" comes into play.

When would the bond mature? For instance, is it a 1 year, a 5 year, 10 year bond etc.? Maturity can range from short to intermediate all the way to long term bonds and all have their advantages and disadvantages.

As always, foreign and domestic are other classifications as well. We'll talk more about how bonds work in the risk sections ahead.

REITs,

REIT stands for Real Estate Investment Trust.

These are companies that own, operate or finance income-producing properties. Those property types include things like apartment buildings, cell towers, hotels, retail offices and more. So, these companies own those properties, and by purchasing shares of a REIT, you own a slice of that company. People look at REITs for the steady dividends they produce from the properties they own which are generating rental income.

But they're typically going to give you little growth. Why? Because real estate doesn't fluctuate or accelerate as fast as stocks typically do. Most of these REITs trade publicly like stocks, making them more liquid than traditional real estate. properties. While there are some liquidity restrictions, it's usually easier to get in and out of a REIT than a physical property. REITs allow you to invest in real estate without necessarily being a landlord. You're basically purchasing the landlord.

Commodities

Commodities are basic goods that can be transformed into other goods and services such as gold, metals, oil, corn etc. Why purchase commodities? Because they are usually a good protection against inflation. No matter how high prices are, these things are always in rotation because they are the raw goods used in many products. They're not going anywhere.

People do still see commodities as higher risk in comparison to other investments such as stocks because of their volatility in prices due to supply and demand.

You can invest directly in the commodity itself, or indirectly through what are called funds. We'll talk more about funds in just a minute.

Cash, Cash Equivalents & Currencies

Holding cash in your bank account is a way of investing. You're investing in being liquid. Savings accounts, Certificates of Deposits (CDs), which are just basically glorified savings accounts with time limit restrictions on when you can touch them, and even Treasury Bills issued by the government are all cash or equivalents.

You can also invest in different currencies, whether it's cryptocurrency or foreign currencies via the Foreign Exchange Market aka Forex.

Funds

Now that we've covered the basic raw investment types let's get into funds. There are Mutual Funds and Exchange Traded Funds (ETFs).

Mutual funds are basically a mix of many assets. It's almost like having a grocery basket and just going up and down the aisles and putting different things in the basket, whether they're stocks, bonds, commodities, or a combination of them. There are even funds filled with other funds!

They're typically actively managed. Meaning, somebody is very mindful about what's going in and out of the basket, and is doing a lot of activity on maintaining that basket. These Funds only trade at the end of the day after the market's closed, and are usually more costly than their counterpart, which are exchange traded funds or ETFs for short.

Like mutual funds, ETFs are a mix of many assets; again, very similar to a grocery basket. But ETFs are typically built to mirror an index such as the S&P 500 and because of that they're more passive. There's not a whole lot of management on that grocery basket. ETFs can trade throughout the day rather than only when the market's closed. This allows for more liquidity and the ability to move more quickly to take advantage of price fluctuations for more active traders etc.

Ultimately, the advantage of funds is the ability to spread out your risk. When purchasing individual stocks, even bonds etc. all of your eggs are in one basket. With a fund, it's a grocery basket. That basket can be as broad or as focused as you'd like. There are literally thousands of funds. Tech stock funds, high yield bond funds, funds with 60% stocks and 40% bonds from the S&P 500. It's never ending.

HOW TO CHOOSE?

So, with all these investment types, how do you choose what to invest in? One of the first things that you want to take into account is risk. An investor needs to understand the risks in order to make wise decisions that align with their goals. There are a few different types of risk, some more prominent than others. I'll explain without getting too deep.

Price Risk

This is the risk of a decline in the value or the price of that investment. I bought the Coca-Cola stock at $20 per share, and now it's down to $15. Price risk typically affects stocks the most. If you've got a fund full of stocks, you'll feel it, but again, the fund helps dampen that risk vs owning just a few concentrated stocks. Things like company earnings, poor business management, the economic environment etc. all influence price risk.

Interest Rate Risk

Interest rate risk relates to the changes in the interest rates in the economy. Interest rate risk is usually going to affect bonds, not stocks. As interest rates rise bond prices, meaning the price you could sell that IOU for, fall and vice versa. Think about it. Rates in the economy for borrowing money are primarily set by the federal reserve. If companies now have to pay 8% to borrow money, your bond that they're paying 6% on is less valuable. Why should I buy yours when I can go get one at 8%? Shorter term bonds are less affected by interest rate changes than longer term bonds. Why? Because in that example, if you own a longer-term bond, that's a long time to have to only get 6% when you could be getting 8%!

Reinvestment Risk

Let's flip that last example and talk about the income from those bonds a bit more. Let's say you bought a bond for $10k that was kicking out 8%, or $800 a year of income. What if you wanted to take that money and double down by buying more of those bonds, but the new bonds were at 6% now. That's reinvestment risk. When the income you earn from your original investment, can't be reinvested at the same rate. Reinvestment risk can also apply to dividend paying stocks or essentially anything that kicks out income, but can't be reinvested back in at that same level of interest it was originally generating.

Default Risk

Default risk is when the bond issuer, whether a government entity or corporation, defaults on their loans. This only happens with bonds and is why it's important to check the grade of the bond before buying. Typically though, if you're purchasing a fund, the managers of that fund have done all of that due diligence.

For the average investor, price and interest rate risk are the most prominent because the average investor is using funds. Funds are built by a management team that's doing the due diligence of evaluating those deeper risks such as reinvestment and default risk. Still, it's good to be aware of these things to help make solid decisions when choosing your investments.

74

Now that you understand risk more deeply, let's talk about your risk tolerance which, apart from your time horizon, is the primary factor in choosing investments.

Risk Tolerance

What level of risk are you willing to take? Things like your age, investment goals, your income and time horizon all factor into your risk tolerance. Understanding the various types of risks and what influences them such as stock volatility, changes in interest rates, etc. help you to determine which investments make sense for your tolerance.

Keep it simple, it's essentially knowing what lane on the market highway you want to drive in. Conservative investors will stick to things like cash, equivalents, and bonds whether individually or, most likely, within funds. Stocks would be minimal, but should always be present at some level because; again, it's a vehicle, and a vehicle will always have both a gas pedal and a brake. This could look like a 20/80 split. 20% on the gas, 80% on the brake.

Moderate, or middle lane drivers will have more of a mix-taking advantage of not only bonds, but also some REITs and/ or stocks. Most likely though, a moderate portfolio will consist of the larger and more well known, or safer, stocks or funds. This could resemble a 50/50 split portfolio or within that ballpark.

Aggressive, fast lane drivers will lean on the gas pedal. they're seeking growth. Oftentimes younger and with longer time horizons. Think growth- oriented stocks over income producing ones, tech sector, crypto, etc.

You can use a risk assessment or questionnaire to help you find your risk tolerance. They're not hard to find and go into varying depths of complexity, but again you can keep this really simple.

Investment Strategy

Knowing your risk tolerance will help you to determine your strategy for choosing investments. Here are some common examples.

- **Growth versus income:** Which is more important to you at this stage of life? A retiree with no salary may be looking for more income than growth. Whereas, a young entrepreneur or professional who's just starting their career may be looking for growth for retirement down the line.

- **Active or passive management:** Some believe that with a more actively managed portfolio, they can beat how the general market is performing. Passive investors just want to match what the market is doing. Where do you fall?

- **Buy and hold investor:** Are you saying to yourself, "I'll just buy it, and sit on it for years like John and his dad? The main thing there is- what's going to be your trigger to sell? You'll need to be decisive on when you take your profit.

- **Socially responsible:** Looking to buy companies that align with your values without sacrificing return as much as possible? Things like green energy or equal opportunity and diversification within the boardroom are some examples.

- **Low cost index investing:** Wanting to keep your fees as low as possible and willing to potentially sacrifice performance to do so by solely investing in indices? This strategy is for you.

- **Value investing:** This strategy is for investors primarily focused on buying great companies at great prices.

- **Dollar cost averaging:** In this strategy, which you can combine with any of the others I've mentioned, you're consistently buying equal amounts at regular periods in order to spread out the risk of buying at the wrong time. An example of this is if you're investing in a 401k every time you get paid.

FEES

How do fees work when you're investing? Here are the main ones you may come across depending on the types of investments you choose.

Trade Commissions

When you buy or sell stock, that's called a trade. The brokerage company holding your account handles that trade, and will charge a commission for the transaction. Trade commissions are typically flat fees such as $5 per trade, or may be calculated based on the number of traded shares such as $0.005 per share.

Mutual Fund Transaction Fees

Exactly what they sound like. They're another brokerage fee charged by the firm for buying and selling specifically mutual funds rather than stocks.

Expense Ratio

These are basically the internal costs of owning a fund. They're charged as a percentage of your investment. For example, .25% also known and quoted as 25 basis points. They're paid to the fund manager(s). Actively managed funds are going to have higher expense ratios because those managers are taking and doing more activity. A reasonable expense ratio is relative to the level of management necessary, but typically 0.5% to 0.75.% is average. Again, it really depends on what level of activity is required of that manager. Most likely, the riskier and more volatile the fund, the higher the expense ratio.

Sales Loads

Sales loads apply strictly to mutual funds. They are a commission paid to the broker or the salesperson. Many mutual funds carry loads to incentivize the broker or advisor to sell them; however, there are also many no load funds to invest in as well.

There's three types of sales loads- up front, back end and contingent deferred. While not overly complex, that's deeper than the scope of this book. The main thing you want to know here is try to seek what are called, "no load" funds when possible.

Management or Advisor Fees

These are typically calculated as a percentage of the total portfolio being professionally managed on your behalf by a financial advisor, portfolio manager or robo-advisor. A safe number to stick with here is about 1% of the assets under management, and is paid directly from the account rather than you writing a check.

So far we've discussed why we need to invest, the basic types of investments, how to choose them based on your risk profile and strategy, and the fees associated with them. What we haven't discussed is the various ways that you can elect to manage your investments once you've built your portfolio. It's one thing to attain it, but maintenance is equally important to preserve, protect and continue building.

As we discussed, when you first begin investing you want to be clear on your goals, time horizon, and risk tolerance. These ultimately come together to help you determine the right investment strategy for yourself while being mindful of fees. But as you continue to build on your foundation, your balances grow, and you continue to age, you'll find that your risk increases. It becomes increasingly important to ensure you are managing that risk, however aggressive or conservative you are. This is done through asset allocation and diversification. If you're not sure what I just said, or what the difference is, keep reading!

Asset Allocation

With asset allocation you're simply trying to maintain a desired mix of assets whether stocks, bonds, real estate or commodities. The question you're answering is how many of your eggs (dollars) are you putting into each of the baskets (asset categories).

Why is this important? Because each of these categories brings with them different levels of risk and return, as well as respond differently in various market conditions. For instance, when the stock market is down, bonds are typically up. Real estate often moves separately from the stock market and therefore can provide some hedge against market risk as well. So while a growth focused investor may largely be invested in stocks, someone approaching retirement may be looking for more protection and income, with growth taking more of a back seat. It's about knowing your lane on the investment highway, and having a process for ensuring you stay in it through strategic asset allocation.

Diversification

Diversification takes things a layer deeper than asset allocation. Whereas asset allocation speaks to asset categories; diversification involves spreading risk out amongst different types of an asset. Let's take equities as an example. Just within that one asset category, an investment portfolio can be diversified across many categories to control risk. Large cap stocks such as Walmart, Home Depot etc. will carry less risk than say for instance, a small cap international stock. While both are equities, the risk associated with them is very different. This is why, I could have a 60/40 portfolio (60% Stocks and 40% bonds) and you could have the same; however, my 60/40 could be much more volatile than yours. It's the same way we both can make a chocolate cake and yours tastes way better. It's what lies beneath the asset allocation, and that's diversification.

Within diversification there can be economic sectors, foreign or domestic, etc. It's all those things we discussed previously in our discussion on investment types. The average investor is not thinking this deeply; and while that's ok when you're first starting out, as you progress, your balances grow and you get closer to needing those funds for income- the conversation and depth of thought on these areas needs to increase. This is why the management of your investment portfolio is an important topic, which we'll get to in just a sec.

Once you've got your asset allocation and diversification how you want and need it- what happens when the market shakes that mix up? Because the market is ever changing like traffic, your portfolio can start to drift out of the lane you want to be in. This is why monitoring and rebalancing becomes important. Monitoring your portfolio entails eyeing your portfolio for areas that are opportune or even detrimental in the long run based on economic, market or political conditions etc. Rebalancing is the process of selling the areas of your portfolio that have gone too high and out of proportion, as well as buying the areas of your portfolio that have gone too low. Again, this is especially important for those nearing the time of needing those funds for income and/ or retirement, or those who are already there. Just like driving on a highway, there's no true guarantee you'll make it to your destination safely, but you increase your chances drastically when you drive defensively and stay in your lane.

So, we've talked about building your portfolio. We've talked about consistently monitoring and rebalancing our portfolio. Who does all of this? Let's make it simple. There's three main ways of doing it.

- Do it yourself

- Do it with someone

- Have it done for you

Do it Yourself - The Self Directed Investor

Want to keep it simple? Taking a set it and forget it approach may be your strategy if you're early in your career or investing journey. This is typically for those who are all about growth, no need for the funds anytime soon. A common way of doing this is by using index funds. Remember, indices are built to simply mirror what a sector of the market, or the market in general, is doing. It's a cruise control approach. Another way is through what are called, "target date" or "life-cycle" funds. These are extremely common inside of retirement accounts such as 401(k)s. They are pre-built funds with an asset allocation and diversification that models the profile of a typical person within an age bracket, or who is looking to retire at a certain time. The fund managers will shift the asset allocation and diversification over time as the target date approaches.

Do it with someone... Most likely, a Financial Advisor

Before stepping into comprehensive financial planning, I worked as a financial advisor. Yes, there's a difference. A typical advisor's role at most large institutions is basically to advise you on your investment account- whether it's a retirement account through your employer that's held with the company they work for, or if it's a stand-alone investment account at their institution or bank. They will take you through an assessment of your risk tolerance, goals etc. to help determine your investment strategy, then assist with executing on that strategy by offering investment recommendations based on their product lineup. If they're any good, you should have ongoing communication with them whether quarterly, semi-annually, or most often annually. This of course comes at a fee which is typically a percentage of the assets under their management. There are other compensation structures they could be under as well-such as commissions on product sales, and so you'll want to be certain you understand how they're paid and why they're recommending certain things. For example, a big one is the class of funds they're recommending. The same fund may offer A-Shares, which pay commissions entirely up front; B-Shares which pay commissions on the back end when sold; and C-Shares which pay ongoing commissions each year you stay in that fund. Often unbeknownst to you, C-Shares typically have much higher expense ratios (internal fees), and that of course, decreases your return.

Have it done for you... Robo Advisors and Portfolio Managers

AI's been in the investment world since about 2008 via robo advisors. There's varying degrees of depth, but it's all algorithms designed by financial advisors, investment managers and data scientists to build portfolio allocations based on data entered about your situation. This approach offers little to no human interaction, and in most cases comes at a lower cost than working with a dedicated advisor which allows a broader audience to receive advice and management. As with anything, there are pros and cons. Minimal flexibility and customization are the big cons with robo advising; but for investors who want more guidance yet don't feel they need the deeper complexity, can potentially benefit.

Professional portfolio management is by far the most in depth and customizable of the options. There are different levels of this in terms of access to face-to-face interaction versus having a team "behind the curtain" approach. But at the highest level of management, there's a dedicated investment manager with a team behind them. Their only role is to build, monitor, rebalance and strategically draw income from your portfolio when needed. Service comes in the form of portfolio reviews, administrative tasks etc. They do not advise on your entire financial situation, that's what a financial planner like myself is for. They simply manage your portfolio, and they do so on a discretionary basis. Discretionary means that the decision making on investment selection, buys and sells etc. are up to them; however, those decisions must fit within your risk profile and align with your goals based on your financial plan. This is ensured through a binding fiduciary agreement called an Investment Policy Statement. At the height of my corporate career, this level of management made sense at the $1M of assets under management mark, and was extremely valuable to my clients who sought out the done for you approach because it allowed them in a sense be the "CEO" of their money, calling the shots at a high level, while delegating the necessary day-to-day tasks to the "CFO," or in this case, portfolio manager and their team. For those looking to build their financial team of professionals- a financial planner, portfolio manager, CPA tax advisor and estate attorney is the pinnacle. This is especially true when they're all in communication with each other. Again those fees are typically calculated as a percentage of the assets under management and will likely range from 70 basis points (.70%) to 1.5% on the higher end.

So there you have it. Those are the most common ways of managing your investment portfolio. Whether you're doing it yourself, doing it with someone, or having it done for you, it must be done. In the investors journey there will come a point when maintenance must be done. It's typically towards retirement, but the size of the portfolio is a huge factor. Managing a portfolio takes a certain level of time, skill and quite frankly-will. If there's even one of those missing, I strongly suggest you consider the 2nd or 3rd option.

One very common question investors both new and experienced often ask is, are your investments insured? The answer to that is yes and no. There's two types of insurance to be mindful of, and both have their limitations.

1. FDIC Insurance

FDIC, which stands for Federal Deposit Insurance Corporation, provides insurance coverage on your deposit accounts which are typically, but not always, at a bank. Think checking, savings, money markets and CDs. It's federal protection of your money up to $250,000 per ownership category in case the bank goes bankrupt and your funds are lost.

So for instance, if you have a bank account with just your name on it, that's going to be protected up to $250,000. But then, if there's an additional bank account with you and someone else's name on it, that's also going to get its own $250,000 of protection.

2. SIPC Coverage,

SIPC, which stands for the Security Investment Protection Corporation, protects against the loss of cash and securities held within brokerage or investment accounts if the firm goes bankrupt and your assets go missing. So, if you have an account through E-Trade, and E-Trade goes bankrupt and your assets within your account go missing, that's when SIPC kicks in.

This is usually going to happen as a result of theft or fraud, and you usually have coverage up to about $500,000. Typically a firm would be bought out before going bankrupt. Also, investment firms are required to have reserves, so there are multiple layers of protection before SIPC takes effect. To be clear, SIPC coverage does not protect against the decline in value of the underlying securities due to the market risk.

In other words, your stocks, bonds and funds etc. are going to go up and down with the market. There's no direct insurance that's going to stop that or protect you from loss. It's only protection for if something such as fraud or bankruptcy happens within the company that holds your account. Still, in these days of major banks going bankrupt it's nice to have.

SUMMARY

We've covered a ton in this chapter. Beginning with why we must invest in order to maintain the purchasing power of our dollars against the threat of inflation and low interest rates, then moving into the typical investment types, or securities. You're now armed with the understanding that stocks move the needle for growth, whereas bonds provide more security and income as the foundation of everything else such as REITs, commodities and funds. Of course there are other alternative investments such as options and futures, but those are derivatives of the underlying assets which are the ones we've covered here. We then dove into how to go about selecting your investments based on your risk tolerance and more, while being mindful of your fees.

But it's not enough to simply build your portfolio. Over time you'll need to perform some maintenance, which calls for a deeper look at things like your asset allocation and diversification. Based on those and your degree of time, skill and will, you'll need to determine how you want to manage your portfolio. Lastly, knowing there's no insurance for the decline in value of your investments is a must. Therefore, our previous chapters around proper mindset, cash management and insurance protection are key before taking on the risks associated with investing.

If you've made it this far into the book, and into your wealth journey congratulations! It shows you're serious about your financial future, and also that you're finding value in this information. I have a request that won't cost you anything but

5 minutes of your time. Would you please leave a review of this book on Amazon? It really helps grow the visibility of the book (and my ego) allowing more people to benefit. Thanks! Where to next after you've begun investing? Well, nine times out of ten, you're investing for later in life. When's later? Retirement, and beyond.

CHAPTER V

RETIREMENT IS A NUMBER NOT AN AGE

It blew my mind to see that retiring had less to do with how much money was saved, and more to do with where the money came from and how it was spent. How could I be sitting across the table from a client with a $3.5M million dollar investment portfolio plus social security income, and still have to tell him in front of his wife that they are going to run out of money in about 10-13 years. There was just no way that they'd have the successful retirement they envisioned if they continued spending at that pace.

Rich and his wife, Myra spent way too much money. He liked leasing out and racing high-end exotic cars, she liked her horses, and they both loved traveling. It sounds like a very nice lifestyle, and it was one they were able to maintain while working. But when you dig into the numbers behind it, it just didn't make sense for retirement and that was a humbling blow to his ego.

It definitely matters, but retirement planning is about more than just saving; and because social security, which has long served as a stable fixed income source, is perilously close to expiration, the stakes are even higher. You must understand that for our parents and grandparents etc. the narrative was to go to school, get a good job, work that job for 40 years- and then retire with your social security and pension. Both of which are guaranteed lifelong streams of income. Not to mention, for those married, if you passed first, your spouse could continue on receiving that pension until they passed as well. So financial security in terms of income was a given. The game has changed drastically because both of those safety nets are almost extinct.

In the early 80's employers began shifting their benefits packages as well as the responsibility of saving for employee's retirements onto the employee via deferred compensation plans such as the 401(k), 403(b), 457 etc. Employees became responsible for having to elect to defer a percentage of their salary to save for retirement, and if lucky enough, hope for an employer who would match their contributions up to a certain point. Those funds are to be invested into the market according to the employee's discretion, and ideally grow for later in life when it's time to retire. The problem is, not every employee is aware of, elects to, contributes enough, or is consistent in doing so over the years. Add this with the inflation and decay of the dollar's purchasing power over a career and it's no wonder we're seeing more baby boomers working longer, moving in with kids etc.

How do we prepare? It's never been more important to focus on building out income streams such as rentals, royalties, dividends, business income, annuities etc. These are all viable options. How that looks for you is obviously going to be different from another, but my goal is to just stress its importance and get your wheels turning for income streams because depending solely on investments to do it is highly unlikely. Here's why.

FINANCIAL INDEPENDENCE RETIRE EARLY

We'll get deeper into how a financial planner goes about retirement planning, but if you wanted to get a quick sense of how much you'd need to have invested to retire at your current lifestyle, take your monthly expense level and multiply it by 25. For instance, if you anticipate needing $5k per month to be comfortable, that's $60k per year. When multiplied by 25, that $1.5M invested in order to retire comfortably. This is called your Financial Independence Retire Early number, or F.I.R.E. That's certainly not impossible, but can feel daunting for the average American who currently does not have $400 saved for emergencies!

Why 25? It's because of the 4% rule, which if you're not familiar, is a golden rule in the financial planning world. It says, never withdraw more than 4% of your portfolio in a year in order to avoid depleting it too quickly. Four percent of $1.5M is $60k. The four percent rule is very rigid and doesn't account for many things such as the fact you'd spend more in early retirement and less in your later years. Nor does it account for the possibility of really great years in the market and the high gains they'd bring. The 4% rule is also based on a 65%/ 35% stock-to-bond ratio, which may be too aggressive for more conservative investors. Still, it's a nice benchmark to look at when beginning to think through your retirement planning at a very high level. But for those that want a deeper dive into a more targeted approach, let's break down retirement planning in a sequential and logical way from a financial planner's point of view.

Step 1: Goals, Lifestyle and the Numbers Behind Them

In my practice, when I work with clients on retirement planning, the very first thing we do is get a clear understanding of their goals. Typically, a big part of most of my clients' retirement goals is to maintain their current lifestyle.

To do so we need to identify their expense level. You've got to understand your numbers. If you don't, you don't have a target to plan for; and as I teach my students all the time, if you don't have a target, you cannot plan. And if you fail to plan, you're planning to fail.

What do I mean by your expense level? To be perfectly clear, I mean how much is going out the door on a typical monthly or annual basis for the lifestyle you want to live. And I would encourage you to separate it in a way that's identifiable. Remember, we discussed your cash management plan back in chapter 2? Needs, loves and likes.

Hopefully, you've eliminated debt at the time you move into retirement, but if not, you'll want to account for that as well. But you'll need that clear understanding on what's being spent and where. It could be as simple as a round figure such as $6,000 a month for needs. Just be sure to factor in the practical incidentals that may not make the monthly budget, but happen every year. Things like property taxes if you've paid off your home; or home repairs, which you can expect to range from about 1-3% of your home's value; or even annual memberships- they all add up. The worst thing you can do in financial planning is either under or overestimate your expense level.

Identify and quantify your loves and likes such as travel, as well as any additional large purchases in the foreseeable future, and you've got a clear understanding of what your financial goals are for retirement. Here's what that typically sounds like:

"Devin, we usually spend about $6000 per month and take two big trips a year, plus some small weekend trips to see family here and there. An annual travel budget of about $10,000 should do it. We want to renovate the kitchen and know that's going to be about $25,000 but probably won't do that for another 4-5 years. I'll end up buying another car in a couple years as well; and since I typically finance with a bigger down payment, I'll probably want to put down about $15k or so on it. Other than that, it's pretty straightforward."

Nothing is exact, but it's again all about knowing your foundation. Once you understand your numbers, you'll then want to assess your current financial situation.

Step 2: What Do We Have to Aim at Those Goals?

What are the income streams you'll receive? What assets and investments are there such as brokerages, IRA's 401(k)s, even Life policies with cash value? Let's start with a breakdown of the most common income streams and the planning aspects that come with them.

Social Security

When it comes to social security, the important thing to know is that, in order to qualify for Social Security, you must have paid into it either through your employer(s) or, for those self employed, through your own tax deductions, for roughly ten years. Those years do not need to be consecutive either.

Ultimately the amount of social security you receive is based on your highest 35 years of earnings.

Spouses are entitled to a spousal benefit of up to 50% of their husband or wife's full benefit, even if they themselves did not work. To receive the full 50%, that spouse must wait until their full retirement age. If they as the spouse did work and paid into social security, they will receive the higher of either their own benefit, or the one they are entitled to as a spouse. This is helpful to the homemakers and stay at home parents. Widows and even divorcees of someone who paid into Social Security may all qualify under the proper guidelines.

Aside from special situations such as being widowed with minors or disabled dependents etc., age 62 is the earliest one may begin their social security; however, age 67 is what is currently considered the full retirement age (FRA). If taken before that full retirement age, the income will be a reduced amount and can be reduced even further if the recipient is still working and earning income over a certain threshold.

Timing when to take social security depends on your specific situation and income. It may or may not be advantageous to early retirees who want to create some level of guaranteed income for themselves and don't want to wait until 67 to do it. But if you're still working into your 60s, it might be best to, at the very least, wait until your full retirement age, where you will get 100% of the benefit you paid into. Lastly, you can delay your social security beyond your full retirement age. Some people may take it at 68 or 69. You can delay it all the way until the age of 70. The good thing is, every year that you delay it, the Social Security increases by roughly 8% so if you delay all the way out to age 70, you can get well over 100% of your Social Security benefit that you would have gotten at your full retirement age. The trade off here is, you're leaving money on the table these extra years, and so you really want to evaluate your health and make sure you're comfortable with that.

Another benefit potentially of delaying your Social Security is if you've got a spouse that you're concerned about- maybe their income in retirement is not the same as yours, or maybe they didn't pay into Social Security at all. Whatever the case may be, there is a goal of wanting to protect and preserve income for them. When Social Security is taken in marriage, if the spouse earning the higher benefit predeceases the other, the widowed spouse will get the stepped up amount. For example, if I'm collecting $2500 from Social Security and my wife's bringing in $1000; if I pass, her Social Security benefit will increase to $2500. However, if I were to delay Social Security until the age of 70, and now be receiving $3200 instead; if I predecease her, she would receive the $3200 instead of that original FRA $2500. This situation often works well for spouses where there is a slight age difference and the income supports not having to take it immediately; whether that means the retiree is earning a pension or has solid investments, or if the younger spouse earns a strong enough income to support the household etc.

As you can see, there's a lot of planning that goes into Social Security. Every situation is different, and again, working with a financial planner can help you evaluate, plan and implement the best strategy for you. It's also important to note that Social Security is taxed. However, for the vast majority of people, only 80% of your social security will be taxed as ordinary income.

Pensions

Pensions are a beautiful thing. As I shared earlier in the beginning of this chapter, Imagine a guaranteed stream of income deposited in your account like clockwork from the time you retire until death. For those married, take it a step further and imagine knowing that even if you passed, your spouse would continue receiving the income until they passed as well. That's about as secure as he gets!

If you happen to be employed with a company that does offer a pension, what's happening is each pay period, funds are being set aside into a fund that is invested on your behalf. If it is only your employer contributing those funds, that is called a defined benefit plan. However, if it's a combination of employer dollars, and a portion of your salary is automatically contributed, this is called a defined contribution. Why? Because your contribution is defined for you, there's no choice in the matter. Either way, these funds are set aside pre-tax, meaning that when you cash in, there will be taxes due since the IRS allowed you to save and invest that money for later down the road in retirement instead of that pay period.

You will want to make sure you know your employer's policy on when it is you become vested in your pension. Vested basically means you have full ownership of the pension benefits. There may be a vesting schedule or number of years you must work at the company before being fully vested. Being mindful of that is key because you could leave money on the table if you decide to leave that company before being vested. For those employed, pay attention to the retirement benefits package or simply ask your HR to be sure.

When it's time to cash in, most pensions will provide you with some options on how you'd like to receive your payments.

Lump Sum

The first option you may receive is to take that pension as a lump sum payment. Be mindful that again, those dollars have never been taxed before. So, while taking a lump sum payment allows you full access to that pot of money, it will come with hefty taxes. In my practice I've not seen many lump sum payouts, nor have I ever recommended a client do so. But as with anything, there's a situation for everything; so, it's an option.

Annuity Option

The next route is to go with an annuity. At its core an annuity is just basically a certain amount of money for a certain amount of time. Annuities can be created from pensions, or sold independently. We'll talk about independently sold annuities next.

When establishing your pension, as an annuity you will have some options. A single life annuity, joint and survivor annuity or period certain annuity. Each of these provides a period of time, whether it's a lifetime or a certain amount of time which is typically 10 to 20 years.

In a single life annuity you're going to receive a stream of income for the rest of your life, and your life only. This option tends to provide the highest payment of income per month or year. The reason being is that it's only for one lifetime. Whereas with a joint and survivor annuity, the income is being guaranteed for the rest of two lives, the retiree and typically their spouse.

Therefore, even if one predeceases the other, the income is still guaranteed.

Within the joint and survivor annuity option there are some selections to choose from:

A 50% Joint and Survivor annuity is when the retiree elects a higher monthly payment in return for a reduced one if they predecease their spouse. When this happens the original payment is reduced by 50% for the rest of the surviving spouse's life. There's a 75% option that acts the same; and finally a 100% option that remains level if the retiree passes before the spouse.

Why do some people select the 50% or 75% option? The thought process is- if one spouse is living rather than two, the expenses are likely to reduce. And so, electing a higher payment while both are living is attractive. As always, every situation is different. It's best to evaluate your own situation, spousal needs, health, longevity, income sources etc. All of these things play a factor in which option you take when choosing to take your pension as an annuity. I'd highly recommend working with a financial planner to help you think through all of those scenarios?

Finally, there's also what's called a *pop-up* option within the joint and survivor annuity. This is applicable if the spouse dies before the retiree does. The retiree's income benefit increases or pops up to what he/ she would have received had they taken the annuity as a single life option. So, the upside is that the retiree will receive higher payments if they outlive their spouse; but, the trade-off is that the initial payments are usually going to be lower than those of the standard joint and survivor options such as the 75% and 50% options. Everything comes down to your specific situation when deciding how to receive your pension.

Regardless of the option chosen, one thing that's nice to have is what's called an *inflation benefit*. Or another way of explaining it is a cost of living adjustment. (C.O.L.A). If the pension plan offers a COLA it can help to offset the effects of inflation by annually increasing the income slightly. Typical COLAs when offered may range from one to three percent annually or sporadically.

Be sure to note that pension income is taxed at ordinary income bracket rates because those dollars have never been taxed before.

Ultimately, having a pension that can account for either some, the majority or all of your retirement needs is an amazing place to be. Imagine 60% percent of your income needs being taken care of automatically. That puts you in a much more comfortable place knowing that you can wake up on January 1st of any year and 60% of what you need for the year is already taken care of, and you'll just need to account for the other 40%. When you combine this with Social Security, which is yet again another guaranteed income, you can imagine the power! For those lucky enough to have worked for an employer that offered a pension (and there are still some out there), it's a great benefit to keep in your back pocket. Just again, make sure you understand when you're fully vested.

Rollover to an IRA, 401(k) etc.

The rollover is a simple concept. It's all to do with taxes. Again. Your pension has never been taxed before. And funds in an IRA,

401k, 403b, 457 etc. are tax deferred as well. Therefore, moving, or "rolling," your funds from a pension into one is a like-to-like transaction. What cannot happen, is your pre-tax funds go into an account with post tax dollars such as your bank account. Those dollars would need to be taxed first and the net amount would then be deposited into whatever post tax account you preferred. This is why again, a lump sum option is rarely used. Imagine your entire career's worth of savings being taxed all at once! So you can roll over your pension, no problem, just be mindful of what type of account you're rolling it into.

What's the advantage of rolling funds over at all? As always, every situation is different; however, there may be more investment options and flexibility within an IRA, which stands for Individual Retirement Account, than within your pension. The ability to take a loan against your own funds within another account, versus not being able to do so within your pension, is another potential advantage. Finally, the possibility of earning a higher level of income on the same amount of money by rolling it over to another account such as a standalone annuity, which we'll talk about next, is another possibility. These are just a few, but evaluating the situation with a financial planner always makes sense.

Standalone Annuities

While pensions offer annuity options, what if you never worked at a company that offered a pension? Or, what if you were self-employed? Apart from the hope that social security is still available, how would you ensure a stable income in your retirement years, whenever those may be? It's a significant problem that can be answered through investing into standalone annuities. Remember, an annuity at its core is a certain amount of money for a certain amount of time. As we dive into them deeper, there are a couple things to note.

First is that an annuity is an insurance product sold by insurance companies with many different options and nuances. Because it is an insurance product there are fees, actuarial projections and contractual obligations associated with them. Being clear about what you are getting into is extremely important and cannot be overstated.

Second is that it's highly unlikely to use an annuity to cover 100% of the income you'll need in retirement. That would take a significant amount of money to be invested. When thinking through retirement planning, it's about piecing a puzzle together to fit your needs and goals. An annuity can, and oftentimes should, be an important part of that puzzle of diversified income streams as they serve a very specific purpose of creating steady, and in most cases, lifetime income. However, an annuity is never meant to serve as the only piece. In fact there is a review process called suitability which is carried out by the advisor and enforced by the insurance company in an effort to ensure that it's in your best interest based on your financial situation including your assets, liabilities, and so on.

Third is that despite the efforts of suitability, annuities are often misrepresented and oversold by financial advisors due to the large commissions they pay. That is exactly why you must understand them at a high level, and build a relationship with a trusted financial planner who can assist you with evaluating your situation to find the right piece and fit. With that said, let's break down the standalone annuity.

Types of Annuities

At their highest level, there are two different types of annuities, immediate and deferred,

Immediate annuities are purchased with a lump sum and meant to turn around in less than one year to start paying out that reliable consistent income. The lottery offers its winnings as both a lump sum, and an annuity. Legal settlements often do as well.

Similar to when we discussed employer pensions, that income can last for a fixed period of years, such as 20 years. Or it can last a lifetime. Obviously, stretching the funds over a lifetime lowers the income amount; but, it provides a different level of security than a predetermined amount of years.

Deferred annuities on the other hand offer more of a growth component to the invested funds with the intention of annuitization at a later point in the future, most often retirement. Annuitization, or annuitizing, simply means turning the invested funds that have accumulated over time, aka accumulation or contract value, into a guaranteed income stream. So whereas immediate annuities will begin to pay out typically in one year or less, deferred annuities are postponing the income until after the accumulation period. Deferred annuities can be paid into either with lump sums, or multiple premiums over time.

Deferred annuities can be funded with post tax dollars as what's called a non-qualified deferred annuity. Non-qualified meaning the funds are not qualified for the preferential tax treatment that retirement accounts receive. In other words, the funds have been taxed before and are coming from your bank account.

Deferred annuities can also be Traditional or Roth IRAs as well. Traditional IRAs contain funds that have not been taxed, and won't be until withdrawn. Roth IRAs are funded with dollars that have been taxed, and are now growing with the ability to avoid taxes upon withdrawal as long as certain criteria are met. From a tax perspective deferred annuities offer the biggest bang for buck when they are non-qualified. Why? Because again, these are dollars that now have the ability to grow tax deferred for many years. Then when retirement comes and the owner is in a lower tax bracket due to no salary, they can be taken out with what would hopefully be minimal taxes. Growth + Lifetime income with little tax = Success.

You'll want to make sure you have a longer time horizon when getting into a deferred annuity. In my practice, I look for 10 years or more before recommending a deferred annuity, and that's for very specific reasons. One is to ensure you're giving the funds time to grow before either taking withdrawals or annuitizing. Second is because annuities have up front surrender schedules. A surrender schedule is typically a seven year period where if the owner decides to cancel the policy, a percentage fee of the contract's value is charged as a penalty. Surrender schedules usually start at 7%, and decrease by about 1% each year until reaching 0% (7%, 6%, 5%...). Surrender schedules are there primarily to keep an owner invested long enough to recoup the commission paid to the agent who sold the annuity.

Do not be mistaken, a surrender schedule does not mean you are not able to access your funds in the first seven years, just that you cannot quit the contract and receive all of your funds back. In fact, annuities do offer a free withdrawal amount each year as well. The free withdrawal amount is also a percentage of the contract that you are able to access each year without penalty. Free withdrawal amounts usually max out at about 10%. It's for all of these reasons and more, that again, you'll want to look at deferred annuities as long term investments.

Within the category of deferred annuities are fixed, variable and index annuities. These options are all related to how the funds grow.

Fixed annuities are straightforward, they grow at a fixed interest rate set by the insurance company.

Variable annuities do just that, they vary. The funds are invested directly into the market through a suite of investment options such as mutual funds or even managed accounts all made available by the insurance company. Because it's the market, the funds have the ability to grow and decline in value over time. It's essentially investing in the market, wrapped inside the ability to switch on a stream of income from the balance at any time you choose. When you do decide to annuitize, the income stream itself can vary because the underlying investments creating that income vary. Most retirees are looking for stability, so variable annuities may or may not be the right fit. However, for younger professionals seeking long term growth while maintaining the ability to create an income stream, the uncapped growth potential may be worth considering.

Variable annuities by far are the most complex of all annuities and carry the most risk. The agent selling the annuity must have both a securities license and be registered with the U.S. Securities and Exchange Commission (SEC), as well as be a licensed insurance agent since the annuity is a hybrid of both the market and insurance. They often carry the most fees as well due to the fact that not only does the annuity itself have fees, but the mutual funds have fees. Going one step further, if it's a managed portfolio of funds, there is the potential for a management fee above and beyond the individual funds within it.

Finally, there are indexed annuities. These are somewhat of a combination between fixed and variable in that the invested funds are placed into an index built by the insurance company that will match an index, or combination of indices, from the market. The insurance company's index is meant to emulate the actual market indices, but it's important to note, these are not the market indices themselves.

This is because if they were the actual market indices themselves, that would make it a variable annuity and thereby no longer just an insurance product, but a security able to decline in value as well. To avoid this, the insurance company places floors and caps on the return the investor can receive from the index. Doing so allows the investor to capture some of the upside of market returns, while limiting the downside. To give an example, an index meant to emulate the S&P 500 may offer a 12% cap, and a 0% floor. Therefore, if the actual S&P 500 performs at a 15% return, the investor will experience the cap of 12% rather than the full 15%. On the other hand, if the actual S&P 500 has a negative year, the investor will not experience a loss in their accumulation value, because the floor is 0%. Capture the upside, limit the downside.

Sounds like a win win right? In many ways it is, but where the trouble happens is again, how they are represented and sold by advisors. Most are looking for the bigger commission and lead with the usual message of,

"You can't lose money."

Unfortunately, when you look at the annuity contract as a whole, that's just not true. Why? Because while the index may not allow a negative return, the annuity contract still has fees and charges built into it; and so, while the accumulation value may not decline because of market return, it will still decline in a bad market year due to all of the fees the annuity is still charging out of that accumulation value. In fact, I've seen the value decline even in an up year because of all the fees. We'll get into fees a bit more but to fully understand, you must also understand some of the other components of annuities; namely, their riders.

Riders are essentially extra features that can be added to the annuity to enhance specific parts that may align with your goals. They are categorized as living benefits and death benefits, and center around income payouts during life or death.

Living Benefit (Income) Riders

Remember that to annuitize means to turn all of the accumulation value into a certain amount of income that is guaranteed to you for either a certain amount of years, or lifetime. Annuitization means you are trading your entire account with that insurance company for an income stream, and it is an irreversible decision. In other words, you no longer own those assets when you annuitize; instead, you now own an income stream. Meaning, if you needed $10k because you were in a pinch, I hope you have it in your bank account, because you cannot withdraw it from the balance within the annuity because there are no more funds available once you've annuitized. This is a major reason why placing all of your savings in an annuity is a major no no, and any advisor or agent pushing you to do so is no good.

Just as with pensions, there are options as to how you set up your annuity income stream upon annuitization. Here's a quick overview

Single Life

The most straightforward of them all. It's one life and one life only. Income will last until death. This usually results in the highest income amount of all the options.

Joint & Survivor

Essentially meaning with a spouse, who then would receive the income either unchanged or reduced. This is the same structure as what is offered when taking the annuity option with a pension.

Life with Period Certain

Meaning the income would continue for the life (lives) of the owner and/ or spouse while also guaranteeing a certain number of years of income payments. This way if the owner(s) passed before the certain timeframe was complete, the beneficiaries would receive the income for the remaining years of the guaranteed time frame.

What if you want the privilege of guaranteed income for life from your annuity, without having to annuitize? A guaranteed

107

minimum withdrawal benefit (GMWB) solves this issue. You can withdraw a guaranteed amount each year without having to annuitize. In addition, the GMWB protects against decline in your contract value due to a poor market whether it's a variable or indexed annuity. Remember, despite the index not allowing a negative return, the fees are still charged and can decrease your balance. With a GMWB in place, if for example you invested $100k and the balance declines to $90k, you will still be able to withdraw a certain percentage of the $100k. The $100k is considered your income base upon which the amount of income you can withdraw is calculated, regardless of the actual accumulated value.

There are some GMWBs that offer a step-up, meaning if the original $100k increased in value to $110k during positive markets, before declining back down, you are guaranteed to be able to withdraw a percentage of the $110k. The nice thing about these is that the guarantee stays in place even if the contract value is $0. So each year, you're able to continue withdrawing, without annuitizing, even if your balance declines or is reduced via withdrawals, all the way to $0. The withdrawal percentage allowed on the income base usually ranges from 5-10%, but you'll need to weigh that out against its cost as it usually adds an additional 0.5-1% each year to your total fees. The higher the withdrawal allowed, the higher the fee. That withdrawal amount can also work on an age band. For instance 51-60 year olds may be able to withdraw 5%, whereas 61-70 may withdraw 7% and so on. All in all, this rider is for those looking to add more security to their income, especially given the variable nature of their accumulation value whether in variable or indexed annuities.

A Guaranteed Minimum Income Benefit (GMIB) is a different type of living benefit rider that addresses those who are actually annuitizing but have seen a decline in the accumulation value due to market decline. When added, the GMIB establishes what's called an *income base* which is simply a dollar amount that your annuitized income amount will be based on. The GMIB guarantees an annual compound interest rate on that income base so that even if the market declines, thereby affecting your actual contract value, your income base still increases. Using some real numbers, let's hypothetically invest $100k with the intention of annuitizing in 10 years for lifetime income, and also add a GMIB rider with a 6% annual compound. If the market performed poorly and at the end of the 10 years your contract had only increased to $125k, your income base would still have risen to roughly $179k. Your annuity income would be based on the $179k and therefore higher. GMIBs typically range in cost from 1-1.5% so again, you must weigh out the cost and ensure it's in alignment with your goals.

Remember, a GMIB is for those who are planning to fully annuitize or "trade" the value of their account with the insurance company for an income stream in return. These individuals are primarily focused on guaranteed lifetime income. The GMWB is for those who want the flexibility of keeping their cash in the contract for withdrawals throughout retirement but understand that those withdrawals will deplete the benefit base. In my humble opinion a Guaranteed Minimum Withdrawal Benefit provides the better deal. You keep your cash and can still lock in a guaranteed income stream, even after the underlying benefit base hits $0.

Death Benefits

Because annuities are focused on income, they're typically not great for financial legacy and estate planning. In fact, most annuities are required to begin paying out by age 90 if the annuitant has not already begun taking funds. If the owner has not annuitized, or is taking lifetime withdrawals through a rider; the beneficiary(ies) would receive a return of the premiums plus earnings, minus any withdrawals and fees. However, if the owner annuitized and is receiving the lifetime income as a single life annuity without a spouse, it would cease upon their passing, and the heirs typically would receive nothing. Remember, annuitization is a trade between the owner and insurance company. Once annuitized, the owner no longer owns those funds as an asset, the insurance company owns those funds; but in return, the owner receives an income stream that typically lasts for life.

Cash Refund

The worst thing that could happen is the owner(s) passes early after annuitizing, and does not live long enough to at least recoup the premiums they paid into the annuity. The cash refund is a rider that allows the owner's heirs to receive the remainder of principal put into the annuity, minus the income already paid out.

Stepped up (Enhanced) Death Benefit

If an owner wanted to ensure the highest death benefit possible, he/ she could add a stepped up death benefit rider. With a step up, the insurance company will take note of the contract value on each anniversary of the annuity, Some stepped up death benefit riders offer the monthly anniversary, others only annual. Either way, the insurance company takes note of the contract value each anniversary in order to provide the heirs with the highest noted contract value upon the owner's passing. There are also those that will step the death benefit up by a certain compounded percentage *or* the highest point, whichever is greater. These are all of course, minus any fees and withdrawals that the owner has taken along the way.

As an example, let's imagine an owner started an annuity with $200k, and over time the accumulation value reached $300k before poor years in the market caused the value to decrease, during which time the owner passed. The heirs would receive the $300k. To take that further, if the owner had taken $30k over the years, the $300k highest balance would be minus the $30k of withdrawals, and the heirs would receive $270k.

It'd be the same situation in the event the insurance company was evaluating which was higher- the contract value on the anniversaries, or a 5% annual compounded death benefit. If the owner held the annuity for 15 years before passing, a 5% compound would make the death benefit approximately $415k after 15 years. That's obviously greater than the $300k highest contract value over that time. However; again going further with our example, because the owner had taken $30k over that time, the amount going to the heirs would be $385k ($415-$30k). That's even though the highest that the contract value had reached from market performance was $300k.

It's important to note that the proceeds from an annuity do not pass to the heirs entirely tax free the same way that life insurance does. How the annuity is established makes a big difference. If the annuity is non-qualified as we discussed earlier, ordinary income tax is due only on the earnings. However, if the annuity is held in a Traditional IRA, all of the funds are taxable as ordinary income. In a Roth, they are tax free as long as the Roth criteria is met. Despite the earnings or the whole pot being taxable, a death benefit, especially a stepped up one, can be a strategic way of adding to your estate. That's especially if you are unable to qualify for life insurance. Death benefit riders can typically range from .25%- 1.5%, which is charged as a reduction to your income payout rate. For instance if your annuity income payout rate were 7%, that would be reduced by your death benefit rider fee.

As a whole the fees on annuities can be steep if you're not careful, which can ultimately nullify the performance of the contract value. What good is it for the contract value to gain 7% if, after mortality and expense fees, administrative fees, investment fees and rider fees your overall annuity costs 5.5% per year? You may be better off investing outright in the market at that point; or doing what's called a 1035 exchange, which means transferring your contract value into a different annuity without losing the tax benefits on your funds in the process. Again, working with a financial planner who fully understands your goals and situation is best to help you find the right annuity and overall investment(s) for your situation. Lastly, do your research on the insurance company as a whole. If an income stream is to be paid for life, you want to ensure the company is in solid financial standing to be able to do so.

There you have it, a comprehensive high-level overview of the types, capabilities, and mechanics of standalone annuities.

Because pensions are almost extinct, retirement income for most resembles a two-legged chair consisting of social security and retirement account withdrawals. If you're needing $6k per month for retirement and social security is giving you $2k. That means that you need enough in your 401(k), IRA etc. to cover two-thirds of your income each month. You're putting a lot of weight on the stock market at that level of dependency, especially if you haven't saved enough over time. This is why annuities make a lot of sense. They are a way to add guaranteed lifetime income regardless of market fluctuations, but there are limitations as well as restrictions so investing all of your funds into one is never a good idea.

How do you know if the annuity is worth it? One way is to understand the payout rate it will provide. If $100k in an annuity will pay you $6k per year, that's a 6% payout rate (6/100 = 6%). Get it? That same $100k in the market would safely give you $4000 based on the 4% rule, but also would come with risk as well as potential for more. It's about evaluating your needs. Covering as much of your fixed expenses with guaranteed money is the goal, and a strong payout rate from an annuity is always a good start. Try shooting for 6%+ when considering an annuity. You can get a sense of this by reviewing an annuity illustration with a trusted financial planner before funding it. If you currently have an annuity, review it annually to ensure it's performing well and on track to provide the income you'll need.

Portfolio Withdrawals

Up to this point in the conversation of income streams we've talked about fixed income sources whether social security, pension, or annuity. Now we're getting into the variable side of income which typically comes from portfolio withdrawals. We started out this chapter by discussing the four percent withdrawal rule, which again says not to pull more than 4% of your portfolio in any given year. The rigidity in this is that it does not account for more expensive years than others; bull or bear markets where there are greater profits or losses to be mindful of; or even higher healthcare costs in later years of retirement. Still, it's a great starting place to shed light on the level of savings needed to create a significant enough income stream to support a retirement.

Building your portfolio up to the amount needed is one thing, and comes from the power of compound interest and consistent investing over time. That all creates accumulation and growth. However, there's a separate layer of consideration when it comes to creating income from your portfolio strategically. Why? Because to create income, means selling the market for cash to deposit into your bank account. Up until needing income, most investors are strictly buying the market. Whether proactively on their own, or through the retirement accounts with their employers, they're buying. When buying, the market cycles work in your favor. When markets are up, investors experience the growth, all while still buying. When markets are down, investors are buying the market on sale; ultimately unbothered by the swings because their need for the income isn't there.

It's different when selling. Imagine needing to create two-thirds of your income to supplement social security, and the market is down 8%, or better yet, 30% in a recession! That's a scary thought that many retirees experienced in 2008. The risk that I'm describing is called, *sequence of returns risk,* and is reflected in the following chart and table.

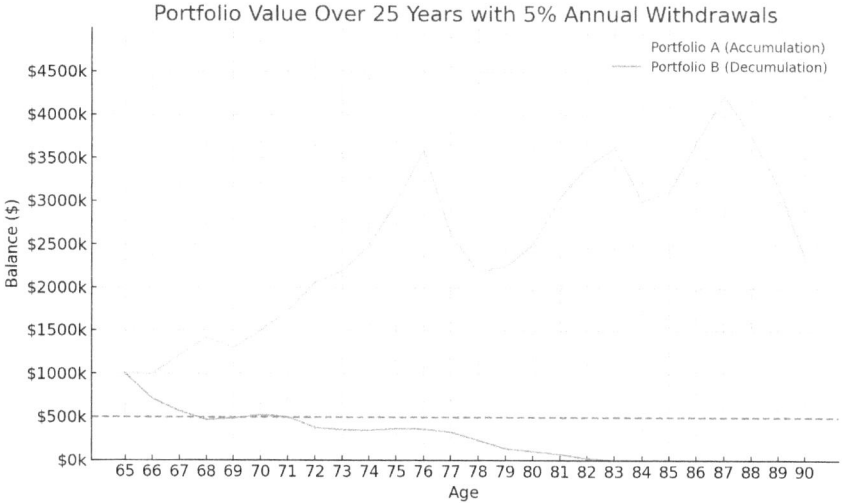

Portfolio Value Over 25 Years with 5% Annual Withdrawals

Age	A Withdrawals	A Returns	A Year-End Value	B Withdrawals	B Returns	B Year-End Value
65	$50,000	5%	$1,000,000	$50,000	-25%	$1,000,000
66	$50,000	28%	$997,500	$50,000	-14%	$712,500
67	$50,000	22%	$1,212,800	$50,000	-10%	$569,750
68	$50,000	-5%	$1,418,616	$50,000	16%	$467,775
69	$50,000	20%	$1,300,185	$50,000	21%	$484,619
70	$50,000	19%	$1,500,222	$50,000	5%	$525,889
71	$50,000	23%	$1,725,764	$50,000	-16%	$499,683
72	$50,000	9%	$2,061,190	$50,000	8%	$377,734
73	$50,000	16%	$2,192,197	$50,000	14%	$353,953
74	$50,000	23%	$2,484,949	$50,000	24%	$346,506
75	$50,000	22%	$2,994,987	$50,000	14%	$367,668
76	$50,000	-26%	$3,592,884	$50,000	5%	$362,141
77	$50,000	-15%	$2,621,735	$50,000	-15%	$327,748
78	$50,000	5%	$2,185,974	$50,000	-26%	$236,086
79	$50,000	14%	$2,242,773	$50,000	22%	$137,704

Age	A Withdrawals	A Returns	A Year-End Value	B Withdrawals	B Returns	B Year-End Value
80	$50,000	24%	$2,499,761	$50,000	23%	$106,998
81	$50,000	14%	$3,037,704	$50,000	16%	$70,108
82	$50,000	8%	$3,405,983	$50,000	9%	$23,325
83	$50,000	-16%	$3,624,461	$50,000	23%	$0

In a nutshell what you are seeing are two hypothetical portfolios invested the same way, both beginning at $1M taking 5% annually as income over 25 years. The only difference is the hypothetical market performance over the 25 years for Portfolio A vs Portfolio B. What you'll notice is that the early years of market downturn in Portfolio B, plus $50k per year withdrawals, really drag on the performance to the point it never recovers. And so despite there being some great years within Portfolio B's timeline; and even though both 25 year timelines average out to a 6% annual return, the retiree is still running out of money in year 20. Portfolio A has the stronger early years which catapults the wealth to a significantly different outcome. There's absolutely no way to time the market and choose the perfect time to retire and begin taking income. However, there are things you can do to protect yourself against sequence of returns risk.

In our previous chapter about investing we spoke on Asset Allocation being an important part of your investment strategy. When planning for retirement and needing to take income from your portfolio, those principles are extremely important. Through diversification it's as simple as creating a situation where you'll have some winners within the portfolio, and some losers. This is opposed to having all winners, which is great when things are good; and all losers, which will really hurt when things aren't. Diversification allows you to sell the winners, while leaving the losers within the portfolio alone so as not to pull from something already down and further deplete your assets. When there's no diversification and everything's down, you're essentially pouring from an almost empty cup. Do that over and over again in retirement, and eventually there's nothing left to pour. Diversification through investment strategy and asset allocation is one of the biggest hedges against sequence of returns risk.

In addition, avoiding taking income from your portfolio in a down market altogether is beneficial when possible. It makes plain sense. So does sticking to the 4% withdrawal rule if you can help it at all.

Last but not least are the income streams. Between social security and portfolio withdrawals most retirees are sitting on a two-legged chair for retirement. Adding more legs (income streams) to the chair is almost always necessary. Even my high net worth and above clients who are able to withdraw the remainder of their needed income above social security from the market still don't like the idea of having to do so. It's too volatile. Again, this is where annuities come into play for their lifetime income guarantee, but any others you can establish are helpful as well.

Putting it All Together

Now that we've gotten clear on our goals for retirement and identified all of our income sources. It's time to put the pieces together. I'm going to simplify this, but of course there are nuances and other considerations such as taxes and healthcare to account for. But, if the goals were about $6k per month as I used in the example, and social security was going to give you $2000-there's a $4k gap to fill. That equals $48k per year which calls for a $1.2M portfolio to stay inside the general 4% rule. Using some of your retirement savings to create an annuity may not be a bad idea to close the gap with some lifetime guarantees. Assuming you're able to get a 6% payout, that'd require roughly $200k to create an additional $1000 per month. Doing so brings you up to 50% of your income guaranteed for life. That's 50 pennies out of every dollar you're going to need, guaranteed. If you're lucky enough to have a pension, the numbers look even better as you may be closer to 70% of your income, or even greater. Either way, it's reverse engineering!

For the millennials seeking early retirement, it's again about finding other alternative income streams through business, franchising, real estate, royalties, etc. With the internet and social media, the amount of possibilities have never been as vast.

Again, this is extremely simplified but illustrates the thought process of a financial planner to a degree. I cannot stress enough that working with a trusted planner is going to be the absolute best way to approach your retirement planning. But having a core understanding and idea allows you to be more knowledgeable, and avoid starting from scratch as well as being taken advantage of.

How & Where to Save

I'm often asked, should I max out my 401k? Should I save into a Roth IRA? How do I prepare myself for retirement, am I on track with how much I'm saving? Here's my thought process on that.

There's essentially three different tax categories you can save within. We'll discuss this deeper in the next chapter, but for now let's simplify them into, tax-now; tax-later, and tax-never. The tax-now category is where taxes on any growth earned are paid in the year it was earned. Ever get a 1099 on your savings account saying you earned $10 in interest for the year. Yep, that $10 is taxable. Accounts such as your savings, CDs, money markets and individual brokerage accounts are all tax-now types of accounts.

Tax-later is where you can grow your money and the taxes are deferred until, you guessed it, later when it's time to take income from them. That's typically retirement, which is why the IRS enforces an additional 10% penalty on withdrawals from these accounts when taken before age 59 ½, which is when they deem *later* to be. Retirement accounts like your 401(k), Traditional, SEP, SIMPLE IRAs all fall into the tax-later bucket.

Tax-never is just that. Funds in this category have the ability to never be taxed again. The one that most people are familiar with is the Roth IRA. However, cash value in a life insurance policy as well as the death benefit of the policy have the same capability.

You'll want to be strategic about how you use these categories to make sure where you're placing your dollars aligns with your goals and timelines. There's no one size fits all because your goals are your own. Just as a good CPA will almost always answer your tax questions, is how I'll answer your retirement planning ones- it depends.

When it comes to saving for retirement, I will say that one effective strategy, especially for those employed, is to start by funding your 401(k) with pre-tax contributions up to the employer match so as not to leave free money on the table. But with this strategy you do not fund it over that amount. Instead, invest as much as you can into one of the following: Taxable Brokerage, Health Savings Account (HSA) or Roth IRA. Which one will depend on your needs and preference. Let's start with the Roth.

Roth

Traditional (pre-tax) and Roth (post-tax) IRA's have an aggregate limit of $7000 per year. Meaning that even if you have a Traditional IRA as well as a Roth, only a total of $7000 can go into them collectively. For those 50 and older it is $8000. However, 401(k) and 403b's are now offering Roth contributions more than ever. This is important because the limit of what can be contributed into an employer account is $23,000; and it is $30,500 if you are 50 or older.

The Roth again is advantageous for its ability to never be taxed again, but that's only after age 59 ½ and at least 5 years of ownership. You'll want to keep this in mind if you are a younger professional starting their career or simply a younger investor period because that means it's money you're designating for a longer time horizon.

Taxable Brokerage

Considering all I've said above in regards to Roth, utilizing a taxable brokerage for the majority of your investing after the

401(k) provides the most flexibility in terms of your withdrawals. This is because you will only be taxed on your growth via capital gains tax (more on this next chapter), and you may access the funds at any time rather than being restricted to an age limit. Of course, if that's not a concern for you, then the strategy changes. As I said earlier, it all depends on your goals.

Health Savings Account (HSA)

Last to discuss is an HSA. These are investment accounts that can be used to pay for qualified medical, dental and vision expenses. They are one of few investments that have a triple tax advantage in that your contributions into the HSA are tax-deductible, they grow tax-deferred, and then may be withdrawn tax-free for qualifying expenses. The list of what qualifies as a medical expense has become more extensive allowing for wider use of HSA's. Examples include copays, medical equipment and supplies, and even insurance premiums. For self employed individuals, the ability to save on taxes in such a large way while paying insurance premiums, which traditional employers usually pay the majority of, can be a game changer in their finances. Visit hsalist.org for a comprehensive list of qualifying HSA expenses.

In order to have an HSA, you must have a high deductible healthcare plan first. Contribution limits per year apply and are currently capped at $4150 for an individual, $8000 for a family, and those 55 or older can contribute an additional $1000 as what's considered a "catch-up contribution."

Given the fact that we will all spend money on our health, having dedicated funds in an investment account that's growing in the market over time, but also allowing you access at any point, provides a ton of upside.

WHY NOT MAX OUT THE 401(K)?

Many reading this will point out the fact that contributing to your 401(k), Traditional IRA etc. allows you to lower your current year's tax liability at a dollar-for-dollar rate. This is another reason why so many contribute to their employer retirement accounts, and even self-employed individuals may do the same through SEP or SIMPLE IRAs or even a Solo 401(k). The idea is, "why pay taxes now on money I'm not planning to use until later?" This is in opposition to paying taxes now on any money that goes into a Roth IRA or Roth 401(k). But again, the ability to grow it tax deferred, then withdraw tax free in retirement weighs heavily. For those who will have high income in retirement, this is even more attractive. Plus, there are other ways to help reduce your current tax year's liability outside of your 401(k) while still setting yourself up for tax free income in the future.

So to review, in this strategy, start by funding your 401(k) enough to get the employer match because you don't want to leave free money on the table. From there, if the "B" word allows, then any additional would go into either an unlimited taxable brokerage, or into an HSA or Roth IRA/ 401(k) up to their respective limits. Which one you choose, will again depend on your preferences and goals. Maybe if you're a couple with no kids seeking early retirement, the taxable brokerage and/ or HSA makes the most sense. Or, if you're a family with stable income but concerned about healthcare costs, the HSA and/ or taxable brokerage make sense. Or maybe you're single in your mid-career and just getting started investing; the HSA and Roth may make the most sense. Maybe even all three after the 401k!

WHERE TO WITHDRAW FROM FIRST?

Ideally in retirement you want to create your income in the most tax efficient way in order to preserve your assets from Uncle Sam's erosion. What that looks like is withdrawing from taxable brokerage(s) first. Second would come your pre-tax retirement accounts such as 401(k). If or when those run out, then shift to pulling from your tax-never funds such as the Roth IRA or Roth 401(k). You want to pull income from the tax-never Roth last because that money is growing with the ability to never be taxed again. So the longer you leave it, the more it can grow, and the greater your tax free income down the line.

This strategy has proven successful time and again. To reiterate, this is only one way of approaching retirement. The reason I highlight it in this book is because the majority of my standout clients in terms of successful, or fully funded, retirements who were also strongly inclined to create financial legacies beyond their lives were keen on utilizing the Roth's capabilities. Even those who did not initially use Roth, but began to in later years, would complete what are called *Roth conversions* within their investment portfolios. It showed me the long term power of Roth even within a wealth transfer situation of passing money to the next generation tax-free.

How much should I be saving?

How much should you save? I'm a big proponent of paying down your consumer debt as quickly as you can. And so money that you would normally invest into the Roth IRA and the taxable brokerage account, push that towards paying off any "bad" debt first. If you're a recipient, don't give up the employer match because again, that's free money on the table. Maybe using an app where debit card purchases are rounded up with the difference being invested into the market is also a good way to invest while paying down debt; but aiming the majority of your dollars at debt is best in order to eliminate it as quickly as possible before investing beyond the company match.

There is no hard and fast rule that says if you save x amount, for x number of years, you can retire. The reason being is every situation is different. You may require more or less money in retirement for your goals than another; you may have a different investment strategy and risk tolerance; and you may also have different income streams in retirement as well. So for someone to tell you a straightforward number, or to say a particular amount is enough for retirement is untrue because it's not grounded in your situation. That said, some general guidelines can help. Again, similar to cash flow management, working on percentages is best. A common framework that I've seen says to retire in 30 years, invest 15% of your income; to retire in 20 years invest 30%; and to retire in 10 years invest 50%. The greatest advice I could give is, manage your expenses through your cash plan, or "B" word (if you prefer to curse); always be working on building out your income streams; and start investing early.

AUTOMATE

One more when it comes to investing. Do your best to automate. Automate the investing from your salary and bank account. I've made the mistake of attempting to rely on my own discipline. Trust me, life will get in the way. Don't leave any room for that. Automate your way to wealth. There are a ton of apps and mobile banking automations that help with this, choose one and get started.

SUMMARY

At this point you've gotten clear on improving your money mindset, developed a cash flow management system that includes some emergency savings and debt paydown. You've addressed your risk management whether through individual policies, or even life insurance with living benefits to cover multiple risks. From there you were able to develop your investment strategy with clarity on your risk tolerance, and have begun putting it into action with the intention of retiring. Where do we go from here? What should you be giving consideration to, or making sure you understand to maximize your goals. In my humble opinion it's taxes, and I'll tell you why.

CHAPTER VI

PLAYING THE TAX GAME

Martin and his wife Rena had recently relocated from Phoenix to Georgia after Rena was having some health issues. To do so Martin sold his private practice as a cardiologist and signed on to bring his talents to one of the largest hospitals in the state where he was welcomed with open arms and a large salary to match. His meeting with me was one of two as he had narrowed down which firm he'd hold his retirement portfolio through, as well as trust with his financial guidance. He shared his financial statements which allowed me to see an opportunity to win his business. A guy not big on small talk and used to tight schedules, I needed to add value and get to the point quickly.

"Martin, you do realize that if you move this retirement account into that brokerage in order to manage it yourself, that's going to create a serious tax bill for you, right?"

"No. My advisor in Phoenix didn't mention that."

"Yep, here's why…"

Needless to say, I won the account. There's three reasons I tell that story. One, I'm really proud of it! Two, is because not knowing or having it pointed out to him would have cost him well over $50k in taxes. And three, it wasn't some obscure loophole, requiring deep tax knowledge to find or see. It honestly only required a very basic understanding of taxes and Martin could've seen it for himself, I just happened to see it and point it out based on what again is basic knowledge. I do realize taxes aren't most people's thing, and that's probably why most are paying absolutely way too much each year.

Let me be absolutely clear before going any further. I am not a CPA. Nothing I am about to share is to be considered tax advice. Also, you should always consult with a tax advisor for more information and to be sure you are doing what's right for your personal situation. All those things being said, I am going to share something that once you read, or hear, you can never go back to the land of tax ignorance again.

Ready?

Taxes are a game. And just like any other game, in order to win you must do two things. One, be on the right team. Two, know and play by the rules. What do I mean by team? Well there's employees, entrepreneurs and investors. Entrepreneurs and investors are the teams winning the game. Why? Because entrepreneurs provide jobs, whether for themselves or for others. For every job they provide, that's one less that the government needs to provide; therefore, tax incentives. What do investors do? They grow their dollars and reinvest them back into the economy. For every dollar they invest, that's one less that needs to be printed; therefore, tax incentives.

These incentives come in so many shapes and sizes by the way. Capital gains taxes, 1035 exchanges, depreciation, business losses and so many more which I'll allow your CPA to advise you on. My goal with this chapter is to simply break down how taxes are calculated so that you have a clear understanding. Why? Because in retirement, more than any other point, taxes matter. Especially when it's your life's savings that's being taxed! To do this I'm going to walk you through the basic tax flow beginning with income.

ABOVE THE LINE DEDUCTIONS

Great job, you brought in $100,000 this year!

The very first thing the IRS is going to look at are your *above the line* deductions in order to calculate your *adjusted gross income.*

Deductions decrease the amount of income you are taxed on. So if you brought in $100,000, and had $10,000 in deductions, the IRS says you've made $90,000 instead. There are two broad categories of deductions, above the line and below the line. What is the line? It's your *Adjusted Gross Income* or AGI. The AGI is the basis for your taxes. It represents your actual income in the IRS' eyes rather than your gross income. There are other tax credits and deductions that are based on your AGI, even loans, government programs etc. Oftentimes the lower the AGI, the better when it comes to qualifying for access to these programs and incentives.

Above the line deductions include things such as contributions to your retirement accounts such as IRA and 401ks; but also contributions to your health savings account (HSA) as well. Other above the line deductions include any student loan interest you've paid and finally, any qualifying business expenses.

Of all the above line deductions, business expenses provide the most flexibility and greatest opportunity for significantly lowering your AGI. Why? It's because the IRS defines a business expense as any expense that is ordinary and necessary to run your business. This is definitely a gray area in terms of what's considered ordinary and necessary. Obviously you'll have a tough time proving that a Rolex is necessary for your business; however, your cell phone, wifi, home office, software, certain subscriptions, security and so much more are easily considered ordinary and necessary. The beautiful thing about most of those expenses is that, they also are in most cases, a part of your everyday lifestyle. So for those running a side business, or even if you're totally self employed, it allows you the ability to deduct a significant portion of your lifestyle expenses from your gross income, therefore lowering your AGI significantly.

A word of caution and clarity, nothing I've said is meant to override the advice of your CPA. Nor is it a green light to abuse the tax code and spend frivolously or claim exorbitant expenses as business related. That's a quick way to get yourself audited. I'd highly recommend good bookkeeping and paper trails of your activity; which, with apps and services, is not challenging to do. That's especially true if you're serious about your business. The following table lists what are just some of the examples of business expenses. You can clearly see how much there is available to take advantage of to help reduce your AGI, and overall tax liability!

Advertising	Office Expenses & Supplies	Business Meals & Entertainment	Software	Office Furniture
Education	Phone & Internet*	Auto Expenses*	Licenses & Permits	Contracted Labor
Subscriptions	Utilities*	Child care	Retirement Contributions	Energy Efficient Expenses
Insurance	Printing	Mortgage Interest	Real Estate Taxes*	Equipment
Legal & Prof. Fees	Travel	Rent	Depreciation	Bank & Credit Card Fees

*IRS expect percentages used to reflect portion of bill related to business vs personal

Let's put this in an example format. Again, you (or you and your spouse together) have brought in let's say $100,000 from your salary(ies), and another $20,000 from your side business. You're up to $120,000 of gross income for the year; but, let's also say you've contributed 10% ($10,000) of your salary to your 401(k); and also had another $10,000 in business expenses. Congrats, in the IRS' eyes you've made $100k, not $120k, because you've lowered your AGI to $100,000.

Utilizing business expense deductions is extremely valuable in the early days of beginning your business, because it's likely that your first couple years are ones where you're taking more losses as you get the business up and running. Just be sure that you're not constantly showing more business losses than gains because the IRS will potentially deem that as a hobby rather than a business, not allowing you to claim the expenses and potentially penalize you as well. They consider it business activity if the business is profitable three of the previous five years, ending with the current tax year that you are claiming your business expenses.

The overall key takeaway I'm hoping that you're seeing is that having a business is a valuable asset when it comes to lowering your tax bill. It also is why working with a tax planner is key. The deeper you get into business, the more valuable it becomes to not only keep good records, but to have a plan about how you will offset the business income and lower your AGI throughout the year. This is opposed to waiting until tax prep time and trying to do so at the last minute. Whether you are a W2 wage earner with a side business, or fully self-employed, there are numerous strategies and ways to legally decrease your taxes; but unfortunately, most people are unaware or afraid based on the hype and lack of understanding of the IRS and tax code.

BELOW THE LINE DEDUCTIONS

You're at $100,000 of adjusted gross income, but it's not time to pay taxes just yet.

There are more deductions we can take before finalizing what our *taxable income* is. Have you ever heard the question, "do you itemize your taxes?" That question is in reference to your *below the line deductions* and there are three types to discuss.

The *standard deduction* is a predetermined amount that the IRS sets based on your household status of being single, joint, head of household, or married couples filing taxes separately. The amount increases just about every year to account for inflation. The vast majority of filers use the standard deduction because the IRS sets it high enough that it usually is greater than itemizing your deductions. Itemizing also takes more work on your part, and creates more work on their part to verify. Currently, the standard deduction for single filers is $15,000, $30,000 for joint filers, $22,500 for heads of households, and $15,000 for married couples filing separately.

If tallying up your *itemized deductions* eclipses the standard deduction for your household, go for it. But if not, then taking the standard deduction makes the most sense to lower your taxable income the most. Itemized deductions include things like deductible mortgage interest, unreimbursed medical and dental expenses if they are greater than a certain percentage of your income, charitable expenses, as well as some state and local income and sales taxes. You can see why most take the standard.

Finally, the last below line deduction to be aware of is the *Qualified Business Income Deduction (QBI)*. It's yet another deduction strictly for business owners, which again blatantly shows us that the tax code is written for entrepreneurs and investors. The QBI allows business owners to deduct a percentage of their net profit after business expenses. That percentage is currently 20%. For example, if the business' gross income was $50,000 and had $10,000 of expenses, there's $40,000 of net profit. The QBI allows the business owner to deduct an additional $8000 ($40,000 x 20%).

The QBI only applies to pass-through business owners and investors, which speaks directly to how your business is structured whether sole proprietor, LLC, partnership etc.

Essentially anything but a C-Corporation is considered a pass-through entity, meaning that the profits from the business pass through to the owner and/ or investor's personal taxes, rather than being treated as an entirely separate tax return.

It is also important to note, that unless Congress votes to extend it, the QBI deduction will expire on December 31st, of 2025.

Continuing where we left off with our example from above the line, our AGI has been reduced back down to $100k. Remember, our hypothetical business brought in $20,000 and spent $10,000 in expenses meaning we have a net profit of $10k. If we're single and take the $15,000 standard deduction as well as the QBI of $2000 ($10k x 20%) our taxable income comes out to $83,000 ($100,000k - $15,000 Standard - $2000 QBI). If we're married it's $68,000 because of the larger standard deduction.

Now comes the tax brackets. Just like the standard deductions, they change just about every year, but there are currently seven tax brackets that your taxable income can fall into depending on the amount. Here is the current year of 2025's in the table below.

Tax Rate	For Single Filers	For Married Filing Jointly	For Heads of Households	For Married Filing Separately
10%	$0 to $11,925	$0 to $23,850	$0 to $17,000	$0 to $11.925
12%	$11,925 to $48,475	$23,850 to $96,950	$17,000 to $64,850	$11,925 to $48,475
22%	$48,475 to $103,350	$96,950 to $206,700	$64,850 to $103,350	$48,475 to $103,350
24%	$103,350 to $197,300	$206,700 to $394,600	$103,350 to $197,300	$103,350 to $197,300
32%	$197,300 to $250,525	$394,600 to $501,050	$197,300 to $250,500	$197,300 to $250,525
35%	$250,525 to $626,350	$501,050 to $751,600	$250,500 to $626,350	$250,525 to $375,800
37%	$626,350 or more	$751,600 or more	$626,350 or more	$375,800 or more

As you can see they range in the amount of income as well as the tax percentage you'd pay based on each bracket, with the largest jumps being the 12% to 22% bracket, and the 24% to 32% bracket. This is the visual proof of why working to reduce your AGI is so helpful because again the above the line deductions are where you have the most control. From there the standard deduction is straightforward, and the QBI is a flat percentage.

For clarity, you would not pay 22% of the entire $83k from our example. Each dollar within a bracket is taxed at that bracket's rate. In other words for single filers, the first $11,925 is taxed at 10% totalling $1,192. The next $36,550 is taxed at 12% totalling $4,386. Finally, the remaining $34,525 would be taxed at the 22% rate to equal $7,595. When added together, the total tax from all three brackets equals $13,173 for a single filer and $7,683 for married couples filing jointly. Compare this to 22% of $83,000 which would be over $18k! This way of calculating is called a *progressive graduated rate* and essentially means the more you earn, the more you pay. The Tax Foundation's video titled, "How do tax brackets work?" is a great visual to help you grasp it on YouTube.

Tax Credits

This entire time we've spoken about deductions, but here's where tax credits come in. *Tax credits* will reduce your liability dollar-for-dollar. Some of the most common credits are the Child Tax Credit for families with kids, and the earned Income Tax Credit for low to moderate income households, which does have an AGI qualifying threshold. Other popular tax credits include the Lifetime Learning Credit for lifelong learners, as well as the Adoption Tax Credit for adoptive parents.

In this example, if the married couple has two children, the current child tax credit of up to $2000 per child would reduce the $7,683 tax liability by $4000, reducing it down to $3,683. Ideally, if the spouses were withholding taxes from their paychecks they will have paid this over the course of the year and not need to pay out of pocket when filing their taxes. If too much was withheld over the course of the year, then a refund would be issued. To be clear, a refund is not an incentive; it simply means you withheld too much and could have had that money throughout the year, rather than waiting until tax time for the government to give you back your own money.

Now you have a clear flow of how basic taxes are calculated beginning with gross income, to adjusted gross income, and finally to taxable income which your liability is then created from. There's tax-paying season, which most are familiar with because of the April 15th deadline to pay your taxes each year. But for the strategic and wise, especially the business owners and investors, *tax-planning* season is what you want to focus on the most. When is tax-planning season? All year! I've received the question as a financial planner so often, "is a CPA worth it when I can use Turbo Tax instead?" Absolutely yes! Having a CPA that's worth their fee can make all the difference in having a major tax liability, or slim to no tax liability at all. A way to protect yourself going into a relationship with a CPA is to ask them to show you what they can save you by working with them first. If a CPA charges $5000 but saves you $10,000, was it worth it?

Unearned Income and Capital Gains

One other area worth mentioning in this book without overstepping my boundaries into the world of taxes are Capital Gains. To go there, it's important to understand the difference between earned income and unearned income. Earned income consists of wages, tips, and self-employment income; whereas unearned income will consist of sources such as interest, dividends, inheritance, alimony, gifts, retirement accounts etc. Unearned income may be taxed differently than ordinary income, which we've already discussed and calculated, depending on its source. For instance, income from retirement accounts is taxed as ordinary income which again is why it's so important to withdraw it strategically in retirement so as not to erode it prematurely. However, dividends paid from stocks can be taxed as either ordinary income, or at more favorable rates called *capital gains rates.*

Capital gains rates can range from 0% to 15% or 20% depending on your household income; however, when compared to the seven tax brackets it's typically lower than your ordinary income bracket rate. The length of time an investor has owned the dividend paying stock(s) will determine whether it is taxed as ordinary income or at capital gains rates. The same applies for the sale of an investment such as stocks, funds, or even real estate.

In the example of stocks, which are simpler than real estate, if you've purchased $1000 worth of stock and it's increased to $3000, you have what's called a *cost basis* of $1000 and your *capital gain* is $2000. That capital gain would be taxed at the more favorable rates as long as you've owned the stock for at least one year and a day. If you've owned the stock for one year or less, you would instead be taxed at your marginal tax bracket rate as if it were ordinary income.

With real estate it's a bit more complex and there are more deciding factors such as if the property you've sold is your primary residence, a second home, or an all out investment property. Again the concept is the same in terms of your cost basis, which would not only include the purchase price, but any related costs such as legal or title transfer fees etc. you paid to acquire the property. But also any money you put into fixing it up. Your capital gains are taxed again based on if they are short term (one year or less) or long term (at least one year and a day).

There are provisions and ways to offset those capital gains, again depending on what type of residence it is as well as if you plan to use the net profit to acquire a new investment property. These are all reasons yet again why consulting with a CPA, and making the most of tax planning are so important. As I started the chapter by saying, the tax code is written for business owners and investors; you want to be on the right team, and also know and utilize the rules to your advantage. If you're not planning to study and digest the 700+ pages of tax code, leverage someone who has!

Summary

Having a basic understanding of how taxes work and how they are calculated really does put you in the driver's seat when making decisions throughout the year. For entrepreneurs especially, utilizing your above the line deductions in a legal, non-abusive and strategic way can allow you to keep more money, without having to acquire more clients. For small businesses, taxes can truly be the deciding factor in success or closure, I've seen it up close and experienced it myself. For W2 earners, the knowledge of how taxes work can help you withhold less throughout the year to avoid a refund, therefore putting more in your pocket throughout the year. For investors, it can be the difference between a large hit on the sale of a property, or having more money to roll into the next one.

Taxes and the IRS are not something to play with by all means, but they also are not meant to be feared and blindly obeyed. Investing in a CPA that not only prepares taxes during tax time, but has the acumen to help you plan throughout the year is pure gold. In the financial world, CPA's are a part of your big three: Financial Planner, CPA and Estate Attorney.

We've discussed the first two, and the realms they operate in. If you've made it this far, give yourself a hand; and give me a review! If you've implemented even one thing from this book, great work! So far we've adjusted mindsets, corrected cash flow, put measurements in place to manage risk, developed investment strategies, planned for retirement, and even reduced taxes. The final piece of a comprehensive financial plan is up next. It's all focused on the fact that you can't take any of this with you when you pass. As a respected colleague of mine, attorney India Ali esq. says, "People die, assets don't." It's because of this that we must have an estate plan. What is that? What are the pieces involved? And ultimately, how do you get one? Let's break it all down in the next chapter.

CHAPTER VII

THERE'S NO GENERATIONAL WEALTH WITHOUT AN ESTATE PLAN

D ominik and Ivana became some of my closest clients over the course of the five years we worked together. They had come from the Czech Republic over 15 years prior to working with me, both as educators. Dominik was a brilliant mathematician teaching at Georgia Tech, and Ivana had retired from teaching at a local middle school. Their adult son Mikal was disabled and would always be dependent. When I met Dominik, his one and only goal was to always ensure that his family was taken care of if something were to happen to him since they were in their later years and all of their family on both sides were overseas.

They'd built wealth, but it was unorganized. Over twenty accounts spread out amongst various investments with no coordinated strategy: cash savings money markets and CD's at multiple banks; little to no insurance; high income, a pension and no wills. Over time, I helped them to consolidate all of their accounts, get long-term care for Ivana and establish a special needs trust that would ensure Mikal could benefit from his parents' assets after their passing, without interfering with his social security benefits.

One day I received a call from Dominik after not speaking with him for some months.

"Devin, I've been diagnosed with an aggressive cancer and I am going to die very soon. I am not sure how much longer I have to live as it is severe. I want to make sure everything is in place."

That's a hell of a phone call to receive. In our final review we discovered he'd had an additional brokerage account he'd overlooked; and by the time we received the necessary paperwork to do something about it, his organs were shutting down in the hospital as his wife facetimed me to speak with him on his deathbed.

"Thank you for helping me and making sure they are ok."

He passed shortly after.

In the aftermath when Ivana came to me with the paperwork for the additional account there was one issue, the account was in his name only and no beneficiaries had been named. This meant that instead of Ivana having access to it, the account must pay out to Dominik's estate, which first had to be settled through the court process called probate. Although she didn't immediately need those funds, it was a serious pain to deal with the process of being able to take ownership of the account. This was especially since all of this was during COVID, and the courts were moving much slower. Ultimately, it took over a year for Ivana to be able to have the account retitled in her name and to access the funds. It was a serious lesson in the value of estate planning that I will never forget.

We speak of generational wealth, yet oftentimes do not understand the elements involved. Currently, almost 70% of Americans do not have a will. Lack of estate planning is even more prominent in underserved communities. While a common reason cited in surveys on the subject suggest that many do not feel they have the assets to justify needing a will- even that is not always the case. How often have we heard the stories of some of our most notable heroes have passed away without what is the most basic of tools for transferring wealth properly?

How often have we seen family members pass, only to leave behind chaos or infighting between siblings and family over assets and how they should be handled or divided?

The myth that estate planning is only for the wealthy is untrue on every level. The very definition of estate planning debunks that myth because an estate plan is a comprehensive arrangement of how one's assets will be managed and distributed in the event of either incapacitation or death. It protects the owner's wishes and their loved ones by seeking to pass their assets on smoothly from both a legal, and tax perspective. Everyone has things, everyone has someone they care about, and everyone will pass, not just the wealthy.

In this chapter I'll break down the key components of an estate plan as well as answer the all too common question, do I need a trust? We'll look at general tax related issues as well as some of the biggest legal issues estate planning can help protect you from. Finally we'll talk about how to go about developing an estate plan for you and your family. Let's go there now.

Key Components

Beneficiaries

Beneficiaries are those you designate to inherit your assets. They can be individuals, entities as well as organizations. Name them on all of your accounts, even the ones that you own jointly with someone else such as your spouse. The power of naming beneficiaries cannot be overstated because they trump the Will and allow your heirs to go directly to the financial institution for resolution rather than having to go through the court first.

Trusted Contact(s)

A lesser known and used tool, but still impactful. The trusted contact is something that many financial institutions use as a way of providing some protection in the event of incapacity without a traditional legal power of attorney. You're able to name an individual who can speak with the financial institution on your behalf. The key here is that this person will only have limited access and abilities. For instance, they may request certain details about the account, but cannot make changes, unlike a power of attorney. It's a nice in-between rather than nothing and no one at all, especially in an unfortunate situation. Ask your financial institution(s) if this is something they offer. You may be surprised to learn it's been available the entire time you've been with them.

Advanced Healthcare Directive (AHCD)

Advance Healthcare Directives provide healthcare wishes and instructions in the event you become incapacitated and can no longer make such decisions for yourself. They are broad and generally apply in cases of illness, injury and even being in a vegetative state. But not in situations of terminal illness or certain death, only when there is the threat of death. AHCDs are documents on their own; however, there are a few other subtypes, some of which aim to be more specific in order to cover a range of situations. The more popular ones include the following.

Living Wills

Living wills allow an individual to provide instructions on the care they'd want as well as don't want after becoming incapacitated. They specifically cover decisions around medical care near the end of a person's life such as, being on a feeding tube, accepting resuscitation, or how long you may or may not want your life prolonged. All living wills are advance directives, but not all advanced directives are living wills.

Medical Power of Attorneys

Also known as *Healthcare Proxies*, medical POAs appoint a designated person to make medical decisions on your behalf in situations of temporary incapacitation such as a medically induced coma. It also allows a designated individual access to your medical records and to have the final say in medical decisions. This is valuable in a situation where there is disagreement amongst family about your medical decisions. Without a Medical POA, again the court has to be involved and appoint someone, possibly a stranger. That takes too much time, and leaves too much risk on the table.

Do Not Resuscitate Orders

DNRs instruct your doctor not to try to revive you if your heart stops beating or if you stop breathing. The doctor will include it in your medical chart. All states accept DNRs

Power of Attorney (POA)

POAs allow an individual to make financial decisions on your behalf. They are able to sign documents, make changes including investment decisions, beneficiary decisions, buy/ sell decisions and more. This person is essentially you, on paper. A common misconception I saw very often in my practice was a spouse believing that marriage sufficed as permission to execute changes on or within their spouse's accounts. Not true. If the account does not have your spouse's name on it, they are unable to touch it. Where typically are the biggest accounts that do not have both spouses' names on it? Retirement accounts. You'd hate to be in a situation where you or your family needs access to your funds due to a medical situation, but have to wait on a court to say yes. The POA addresses that. A Power of Attorney can be *springing,* or *durable.*

Springing means it is not in effect until you become incapacitated. At that point it "springs" into action, allowing your POA to move on your behalf.

Durable simply means it's in effect at any and all times. Choose wisely. In divorce, POAs, especially durable ones, are the quickest to be changed.

It is important to note that when choosing a financial power of attorney, you'll want that individual to have knowledge of where your assets are, access to passwords etc. I can't tell you how many situations I've seen where a person is named as financial POA for someone, yet had no clue what company to reach out to, who to call or even what assets were owned. If you're going to name them as POA, a conversation needs to be had about where and how they can access your funds. In addition, you'll want that person to have a level of financial acumen to handle your finances wisely. In other words, don't name someone who is known to make poor financial decisions, simply because they are a loved one. In my practice, I saw many of my clients name their son as the financial POA, and their daughter as the medical POA as they felt each would make better decisions on their behalf in those respective areas. This is just one example, but ultimately what I am saying is choose wisely.

Lastly, designate a successor. It is possible to name a successor POA in case the first person is either deceased or incapable. This is smart for married couples especially because typically spouses will name each other as the first POA. Having a backup already named just in case is extremely wise and costs you no extra time or money to do.

Last Will & Testament (Will)

A Last Will and Testament, or Will for short, is a legal document providing instructions on how to manage and distribute your assets in the event of your passing. It also designates your executor, or executrix. This is the individual responsible for carrying out those wishes and representing your estate in court throughout the probate process.

Probate is the legal process that occurs after death in which your estate is settled by paying back creditors who have made claims against your estate for any outstanding debt, as well as distributing the remaining assets. This happens according to the will, if there is one, or according to the decisions of the court if there is not one. The formal transfer of those assets to your heirs after any creditors is what is meant by the phrase, settling your estate. This process can be fairly straightforward, or can be a long and drawn out process depending on many things including the size of the estate, the beneficiaries and creditors involved, any appraisals needed on valuable items, the court itself and so much more.

Many times families will hire a probate attorney to assist with the probate process and all of the paperwork. If any property such as land or real estate was owned outside the state of residency, probate within that state of ownership must be done as well. Between probate attorney fees, the time and paperwork involved, probate can be very draining from a time, energy and financial perspective if estate planning is not done on the front end to help smooth out the process. A will can help in doing so by giving the court clear instructions on your wishes, guardianship of minor children and your assets.

At the same time what this also means is that, without a will, the court has no instructions or representative for addressing the guardianship of any minor children if applicable, or your estate; and will therefore have to decide and appoint someone. That person and those decisions may not always be what you would have wanted. This is why having the will and naming a trustworthy and responsible executor is so important. Executors can be close relatives, friends, accountants, attorney's, or even financial institutions that serve as professional executors.

Be clear, the will only becomes active in death, not incapacitation. Again 70% of Americans do not have a will according to many studies on the topic. With the baby boomer generation set to pass over $70 trillion to their heirs over the next 20 years in the greatest wealth transfer this country has seen, leaving assets exposed to the legal system is not ideal. Even if it's a small $30,000 house from Grandma, or a couple acres of farmland, it still has value. That value can be both sentimental and financial, and cannot afford to be put into the wrong hands.

By now you can clearly see the importance of the will. But for many, there is deeper planning and greater protection sought after. The idea of avoiding the probate process altogether is appealing, as well as other advantages that all come to the forefront when considering a trust. Let's go there next.

TRUST

A Trust is an entity, meaning that on paper it exists the same way a person or a company does. Therefore it has the ability to own assets, and to purchase and sell them as well. Trusts provide the highest level of estate planning, protection and anonymity for you and your family. The degree of thought, instruction and safeguarding that you can put around your assets for your heirs and even the generations beyond them is almost limitless. Assets within a trust avoid probate. That is one of the most immediate and attractive benefits of a trust, but there is much more. Before getting into its advantages and capabilities, let's first break down exactly what a trust is, as well as the types.

Components of a Trust

- **Grantor-** The individual creating the trust and granting it with assets.

- **Trustee-** The individual(s) or even company entrusted with the fiduciary responsibility of executing on the instructions of the trust. Similar to the Power of Attorney, naming a successor trustee is extremely wise.

- **Beneficiaries-** Those who will benefit from the trust

- **Assets-** It's not enough to have a trust, you must fund it with assets. Trusts can open bank accounts, investment accounts, own property, life insurance policies and so much more.

- **Terms-** The terms of your trust is where your degree of thought and creativity come to the forefront. Limitations, qualifications, and timeframes for accessing funds etc. are all at play. Ensuring that those benefiting from the trust cannot abuse the privilege by requiring certain qualifications are met first is a great form of protection and preservation. For example, the requirement that one must have held a job for two years and have a credit score of 650 prior to requesting a distribution from the trustee is a possibility. Disclosing the purpose of the funds requested to the trustee in order to ensure alignment with the requirements of the trust is also a possibility. Again, it's limitless. Instructions and stipulations such as these along with the methods in this book that I've discussed are how wealthy families have not only established wealth, but preserved it over generations.

Now that the components are clear let's discuss the types and their purposes.

Types of Trusts

Revocable (Living) Trust

A Revocable Trust is one that is established and able to be changed, or even terminated, while the grantor (you) is still living. When established, the grantor typically names themselves as the trustee as well. Naming a successor trustee in case of incapacity is a wise thing to do. Once established, as trustee, you may use the trust to open accounts, name the trust as beneficiary on your life insurance and retirement account(s), transfer assets such as your home into the name of the trust etc.

None of this will affect you tax-wise as the revocable trust is a pass-through entity. If you recall from our tax chapter, this simply means any and all tax implications such as income that the trust generates, deductions and credits will all pass through to the grantor on their individual tax return. This makes things simple from a tax perspective, while still giving you full control and the legal protection you are looking for. Upon death and (depending on your instructions) incapacitation; the revocable trust becomes irrevocable. This means it can no longer be modified or terminated, it's locked in, and the terms you've set in place must be followed. At this point the successor trustee steps into place to carry out those wishes. Hiring a corporate trustee can be extremely beneficial when thinking long-term. At my last firm this was an attractive selling point for our professional management of assets. Having a portfolio manager to handle the daily investment management activities, a financial planner to oversee all aspects of a client's wealth strategy, and the firm serving as corporate trustee to manage the trust in the event the client became incapacitated or deceased provided a level of security for our high net worth clients unmatched by much of our competition. Revocable trusts are the most common for the benefits they provide while still maintaining control.

Irrevocable Trust

An Irrevocable trust cannot be changed or modified. It stands apart from the grantor upon its establishment as its own entity, with its own Tax ID number and tax return called a K-1, that must be filed annually. Why establish one while living? The answer is typically tax related. When assets are moved into an irrevocable trust they are no longer owned by the grantor, but instead the trust. A grantor who does this is most often seeking to lower his or her taxable estate, by shifting ownership of assets. Either that, or they are looking for asset protection from legal issues such as being sued or divorce.

Currently there is a threshold of $13.61M in value that if reached, your estate would be taxed upon your death for any amount over the threshold. When a grantor gifts assets such as real estate into the irrevocable trust, he or she is trying to reduce the value of their estate, especially knowing that the property will continue to appreciate in value, ultimately costing their heirs significant taxes via the estate tax upon their passing.

Another possible reason is to have the income an asset is producing be taxed at a lower bracket by having the beneficiaries in a lower tax bracket receive the income rather than the grantor. In this case, again let's assume it's cash-flowing real estate and the grantor is in the highest tax bracket. The grantor may give that property to the irrevocable trust, allowing the trust to pay out to the beneficiaries who would likely be in a lower tax bracket. Now they've lowered the taxes on their estate; protected their assets from litigation such as being sued or being subject to divorce proceedings, therefore keeping it in the family; and, provided income to their beneficiaries that's being taxed at a lesser amount than if the income were going to the grantor.

Hopefully this provides some clarity at a high level view as to why establishing an irrevocable trust can be extremely valuable if the net worth supports it. For most, the revocable trust accomplishes the grantor's goals; however, remember that revocable trusts do become irrevocable upon death, and sometimes incapacity.

Ultimately, there are various types of trusts which solve very specific goals such as Charitable Lead and Charitable Remainder trusts for philanthropic endeavors; Generation Skipping Trusts, designed to avoid estate taxes when both the parents and children pass away, all in an effort to benefit the grandchildren. Parents of disabled children would be wise to understand more about Special Needs Trusts, designed to assist those with special needs without interfering with their public assistance such as medicaid or supplemental security income (SSI). Still, each of these will fall under either revocable, or irrevocable which is why having clarity on your goals with your estate is so important.

Do I Need A Trust?

By all means, going straight to your estate attorney to begin developing your plan is not a bad idea. However, over the years the clients I saw that had the most success with their estate planning first worked with a financial planner in order to gain more clarity over their finances and goals. This allowed them to have deeper conversations with their attorney rather than starting from scratch and making decisions, only to be referred to a planner, then needing to go back and make costly amendments to their estate documents.

As planners, we are constantly asked the question, "do I need a trust?" I typically answer that question this way– if there's a family situation or dynamic you want to protect your assets from such as a blended family, a spendthrift child, or possible divorce etc. that can be a major call for a trust.

Assets that would likely go through probate such as jewelry, art, vehicles, investments or a home, especially in multiple states is another red flag.

If you prefer to establish and enforce clear guidelines about not only how the assets are distributed, but when and how they are used, you're likely going to benefit from a trust.

The list goes on. Ultimately, a trust provides you with a certain level of control from the grave that simply having a will just won't do. This is not to say that everyone needs a trust. One setback, depending on perspective, is that they can be costly. Depending on the complexity of your assets and overall situation, trusts can become expensive to draft, review, maintain and fund. They can also become time consuming from an administrative perspective, especially for those with sizable assets such as real estate portfolios or multiple businesses needing documents, deeds and accounts to be retitled etc.

If your estate is small and uncomplicated, there's no family dynamics to navigate and your will going into the public record is not a major concern–you may not need a trust. Oftentimes, single individuals with no children do just fine with a will. If mom and dad own a home, a vehicle and have some savings which are all simply meant to be split down the middle–wills may suffice.

On that note it is important to mention that each spouse in a marriage requires their own wills, POAs and advanced directives etc. Trusts can be joint or individual; deciding which is best would be a matter of preference and planning.

GIFTING

Up to this point, we've discussed financial legacy from the standpoint of death; but it is just as impactful, if not more, to create a financial legacy *during* life. Gifting is something that many of my clients have mastered the art of. In fact, this book would exist differently had it not been for generous gifts. Whether it's to family, organizations, causes, alma maters and more, gifting during life allows one to see the impact of your goodwill, and to also ensure your seeds grow and funds are used as intended. Gifts may be liquid cash, stocks or even property– and there are a couple keys to be mindful of when doing so.

It's important to note that for the donor, giving to individuals can be taxable once the gift exceeds certain limits. For the recipient individual, there are no taxes involved in most cases. When gifting to qualified charitable organizations such as churches, universities etc. the funds are tax deductible; however, they are considered below-the-line deductions, and the filer must itemize their deductions in order to take advantage. This means that if your itemizations do not exceed the standard deduction for your household, it's still best to take the standard deduction.

Stock and property owned over one year that has appreciated can be gifted while providing some great tax benefits for the donor as well as the charity. By gifting appreciated assets, the donor avoids realizing the gains of those assets and having to pay the capital gains tax liability. Instead, the donor may deduct the entire value of that asset, while simultaneously making an impactful gift.

For example, if a donor bought 100 shares of stock at $20 per share, their cost basis is $2000 ($20 x 100= $2000). If the shares increase to $50, the donor's market value is now $5000, and he/she has an unrealized capital gain of $3000. At a 20% capital gains tax rate, the potential tax liability would be $600 if they were to sell the stock. However, if the donor chooses to donate the stock, they've made a gift of $5000 that can be an itemized deduction on their taxes– and the organization receives $5000, rather than $4400. This is why donating appreciated stock can be valuable as a part of a gifting strategy, especially when seeking ways to lower the value of an estate or a tax liability.

Donations from an Individual Retirement Account (IRA) of pre-tax funds are a great way for individuals to avoid income if not needed, and the tax liability it comes with. This is all while making an impact through a charitable organization. This process is called a Qualified Charitable Donation, or QCD for short. For individuals who have enough income in retirement, but are seeking ways to gift and/ or lower their estate, or simply make an impact– QCDs are a viable option. This is especially true when the donor is of Required Minimum Distribution age, which calls for a certain minimum of the IRA funds to be drawn from the IRA regardless of need.

As you can see, estate planning is a loaded conversation that requires much thought and planning. This is because when doing so, you're considering relationships, goals, balances, timeframes, desired impact, and even taxes.

Taxes on an estate became even more of a topic to consider at the forefront of estate planning after the SECURE Act legislation was passed in 2019. A prominent factor in why is because it drastically changed how inherited retirement accounts are taxed. With over half of American families holding some level of their investable wealth in retirement accounts- how those assets are taxed upon transfer to heirs cannot be ignored.

In the past, when a retirement account such as a 401(k), IRA etc. was inherited by anyone other than a spouse, those individuals were typically required to withdraw a calculated minimum amount each year. The investment account could remain intact and invested in the market with the ability to continue to grow- only a minimum withdrawal for tax purposes. This allowed a greater chance at tax deferred growth for life and ultimately generational wealth; however, not anymore. Now, when inherited, retirement accounts must be emptied within a 10 year timeframe. Think about the impact- the growth is limited, the taxes are sped up and the perpetuation of wealth is drastically impaired. Simply put, with no plan, the impact of taxes alone on what may likely be an individual's life savings are eroded by approximately one-third in taxes as their children inherit them.

When this legislation passed, life insurance became an even greater solution for wealth preservation. Why? Because the tax-free death benefit immediately replaces those unavoidable taxes on the retirement accounts left behind. The question then becomes, how does one know how much the anticipated taxes will be in order to assess how much life insurance they'll need? The answer, again- work with a financial planner.

Summary

Designing your estate plan is multilayered depending on all of the above referenced aspects and nuances. But one thing is for certain- estate planning is not strictly for the wealthy, it's for everyone. Without it, you are subjecting your loved ones to a greater level of time, stress, energy and money that they will pay for your lack of planning.

Working with a financial planner first helps clarify your goals, capabilities, and projections. It arms you with the necessary tools to have thorough conversations with an estate attorney. Your will, power of attorneys and advanced healthcare directives will come standard with just about all estate attorneys. However, when diving into the terms of your trust(s), you'll have the flexibility to design something that suits your wishes, stays mindful of potential taxes and protects both you and your family for years to come.

CHAPTER VIII

PUTTING IT ALL TOGETHER

Everything is created twice. First in the mind, then in "reality." Your current financial situation is no different. If you're proud of where you currently are- congrats. But if not, here's the good news. Your future financial situation is created the same way. This is exactly why the first chapter of this book delves into your mindset. From the beliefs you didn't even know you had and the financial trauma you may have experienced, to the vision you wrote with conscious thought, and the intentional affirmations you're using to help you stay on track. Mindset is inarguably where your financial freedom begins, but your actions are where it will be built.

The very first thing you must do is implement a cash management system. An entrepreneur I respect once said that the word system really is an acronym that stands for Saving YourSelf Time Energy & Money. Without a system for how you manage your dollars, your dollars will manage themselves- and you. They will manage your emotions, your opportunities, and ultimately your life. Been there- not fun. Your system needs to be simple and one you can both easily communicate, as well as automate where necessary (i.e. saving). Bad debt is the enemy of wealth. If the debt does not create more assets or positive cash flow, it's bad debt. There's six choices when it comes to bad debt-negotiate for lower rates, consolidate for easier management, snowball for speed, avalanche to save, cash flow index to focus on cash flow, or bankruptcy to start over. Choose one and get to it. Leave your pride, ego, guilt and shame at the door when you do because this whole country operates in debt, so you're not a special case of poor money management or whatever other story is running through your mind. The sooner you get the debt under control the sooner you can start building wealth, but make sure you're protected with the proper insurance first.

Disability and life insurance are just shy of mandatory in almost every situation. The numbers don't lie, if adults are five times more likely to become disabled than die prematurely– and 44% of bankruptcies are due to loss of income from a medical condition, and 37% of Americans do not have the savings to cover a $400 emergency- how can you afford not to have it? Most employers offer disability in some capacity, life insurance as well. Having your own of each, outside of your employer is a best case scenario since your company policies are not portable- meaning if you leave, they're gone. Oftentimes, the life insurance through an employer is not enough either.

For business owners, the conversation is even more serious given the fact that the business depends on you. Do not skip over this important step of managing life's risks in your wealth journey whether you are a wage earner in your profession or an entrepreneur. It is only after the necessary protection is in place that your focus should turn to investing.

Whether you start a business, buy a business, purchase real estate or precious metals, investing is necessary to grow your money. Inflation is as high as it's been in 40 years and price gouging has made its way to the political stage. Bank interest rates are laughable. There is no choice. Take the time to understand the risks so that you can properly assess your tolerance, and develop your personal strategy. Funds will often provide more safety than individual securities because of their ability to diversify your funds, even if it is within one sector of the market. There is no getting rich quick, investing is a long game, but don't allow that to discourage you. Remember, in the average decade, 7 of the 10 years, the market is positive and three are negative- we just don't know which will be which. Your ability to stay invested and stick to your strategy (i.e. stay in your lane) will be the largest deciding factor in how well you do over time.

When it's time to create income for your retirement whether at 70 years old, or 50- the rules are about the same. Income streams, especially guaranteed, are best- and excessive taxes are the worst. Find ways to build out your income streams while working. Passive income is ideal and necessary as it has no ceiling. But there's only so much activity you can do to continue creating income. For millennials, looking to social security for lifetime income in retirement is dangerous, and pensions are being offered less and less. Annuities serve a particular purpose for creating income, but come with potential fees, restrictions and stipulations that can be detrimental without a complete understanding. Working with a financial planner is best to ensure you piece your retirement income puzzle together strategically. Always remember the 4% withdrawal rule from your investment portfolio as a starting point for your calculations; and again, be sure to understand the tax implications of each income stream you receive.

There's a reason CPA's are highly paid professionals. Finding ways to minimize your taxes is fully legal and fully encouraged. Above the adjusted gross income line is where you'll have the most flexibility, which comes through real estate investing or business ownership- it's how the tax code is written. Below the line is where your standard or itemized deductions live, and your taxable income is calculated from there using the current seven tax brackets along with your household status as single, married or head of household. Any credits able to be taken advantage of will assist dollar-for-dollar with reducing your liability, and a refund means you've paid too much. Positioning your assets to be tax-smart is a wise thing to do as early as possible. There's assets taxable in the year you realize the growth, tax deferred vehicles such as your 401(k) or Traditional IRA, and finally the tax never category where your assets can escape Uncle Sam altogether. Your financial planner can help you assess what you have, where it is and if it's best to reposition it.

Every word of this chapter is for nothing without an estate plan. A mentor of mine shared how each year around his birthday, he reviews and updates his estate plan and documents. New passwords go down on the list, the power of attorney gets a phone call, adult children get updated and documents get reviewed. Why, I asked. His reply, "because if I say I love them, how could I leave them with my mess when I die?"

Speechless.

This has been, The Wealth Blueprint. Thank you for reading, but without application, nothing changes. Take it in bites, it will not happen overnight. Everyone is on their own journey. If you've made it here, you owe it to yourself to implement something you've learned- and you owe me a review!

Thanks so much.

God bless!

ABOUT THE AUTHOR

Devin Alphin is a licensed wealth manager with over a decade of experience helping high-net-worth professionals and entrepreneurs build and protect their wealth. Specializing in retirement planning, he combines proven strategies with an understanding of the psychological aspects of money management. As a sought-after speaker and educator, Devin also teaches financial literacy to youth, empowering individuals to achieve financial independence and create lasting legacies. He lives in Georgia with his wife, two sons, and their family dog.

Learn more and access additional resources by visiting **www.DevinAlphin.com**

www.ingramcontent.com/pod-product-compliance
Lightning Source LLC
Chambersburg PA
CBHW060931220326
41597CB00020BA/3511